POINTS *of* VIEW

POINTS *of* VIEW

Aspects of Present-Day English

ROBERT BURCHFIELD

Oxford   New York

OXFORD UNIVERSITY PRESS

1992

Oxford University Press, Walton Street, Oxford OX2 6DP

Oxford New York Toronto
Delhi Bombay Calcutta Madras Karachi
Petaling Jaya Singapore Hong Kong Tokyo
Nairobi Dar es Salaam Cape Town
Melbourne Auckland

and associated companies in
Berlin Ibadan

Oxford is a trade mark of Oxford University Press

First published as an Oxford University Press
paperback 1992

British Library Cataloguing in Publication Data
Data available
ISBN 0-19-282943-2

Library of Congress Cataloging in Publication Data
Burchfield, R. W.
Points of view : aspects of present-day English / Robert
Burchfield.
p. cm.
1. English language. 2. English language—Grammar—1950–
3. English language—Usage. I. Title.
420'.904—dc20 PE1072.B793 1992 91–46213
ISBN 0-19-282943-2

Typeset by Hope Services (Abingdon) Ltd.
Printed in Great Britain by
Biddles Ltd.
Guildford and King's Lynn

For Jenny, Jon, and Liza
and my grandchildren
who will help to carry
the English language
forward into the twenty-first century

Ours is a Copious Language, and Trying to Strangers.
(Mr Podsnap in Dickens's *Our Mutual Friend*, 1865)

But empiricism, decent Western empiricism, honest truth-bearing ordinary language, *that's* what we've got to save.
(Iris Murdoch, *The Message to the Planet*, 1989)

The publishers are grateful to John Benjamins Publishing Company, Amsterdam, for permission to reproduce 'The Fowler Brothers and the Tradition of Usage Handbooks', and to *The Sunday Times* for permission to reproduce articles in Parts 3 and 4 of this book which originally appeared in its 'Words and Meanings' column.

Preface

Towards the end of 1987 I was invited by the Literary Editor of the *Sunday Times* to contribute a regular 'Words and Meanings' column of approximately 800 words to the Books Section of the paper. The invitation could not have come at a more opportune time, as I was in the process of sorting out my ideas for a formidable task that I had undertaken—the preparation of a new version of H. W. Fowler's celebrated book *Modern English Usage*, first published in 1926. The writing of these articles has provided me with the chance to give a public airing to some of the central problems of English usage. There has been a considerable response from readers of the *Sunday Times*, and I am immensely indebted to all the people who have written to me about particular points of grammar or vocabulary. Extracts from a few of the substantial numbers of letters I have received are printed here at the end of the essays to which they belong.

Details of the original date and place of publication of each of the essays—some of which were published elsewhere than in the *Sunday Times*—are provided at the end of each essay. A few of the essays appear here for the first time. I have also included two longer essays, one of which first appeared in 1991 in a collection of papers (published in Amsterdam) on English traditional grammar; and the other in *Fair of Speech: The Uses of Euphemism*, edited by D. J. Enright (Oxford University Press, 1985), now out of print.

It is never an easy matter to establish the status of elements of the language at any given time, and the present time is no exception. In the circumstances in which he worked—far from great libraries and their burgeoning collections of learned journals and academic monographs—H. W. Fowler depended most heavily on the language as he found it presented in newspapers (especially *The Times* and the *Daily Telegraph*) and in a limited range of mostly eighteenth- and nineteenth-century authors (see p. 6). He gave scant attention to American English and none whatever to varieties of English further afield. It is remarkable that a work of such majesty and authority should have as its basis a small personal library of cherished works and the newspapers that he (and his brother until his death in 1918) scrutinized with such care.

For my part I have depended most heavily on a substantial corpus of illustrative grammatical and lexical material that I have built up myself from works written in the 1980s and early 1990s, filed partly in an Apricot personal computer and partly in card-index form. When it was relevant to do so, I have gone to considerable trouble to establish the currency and standing of particular matters of English usage in overseas English-speaking countries, especially the United States.

I have also tried to keep abreast of the immense amount of scholarly work on the language and on theoretical linguistics in the twentieth century. To anyone with eyes to see, the gap between the complexities and the conclusions of this scholarly work and the sturdy and virtually invincible attitudes and beliefs of ordinary standard speakers of the language is really quite startling. The important theoretical work now being presented in learned papers and monographs and at great linguistic conferences is a world away from the day-to-day usage problems that are resolved by ordinary people from treasured and tattered old works of reference and from deeply embedded prejudices. My role in this book, as I see it, is that of a mediator between two widely separated groups.

The essays in sections 3 and 4, it will be observed, are arranged in alphabetical order, not thematically. It is doubtless self-evident that they deal with just some of the areas of English usage that are or have become controversial in varying degrees. For reasons of space I have used an abbreviated system for citing sources: (Iris Murdoch, 1987) should be understood to mean a novel by Iris Murdoch published in 1987, in this case *The Book and the Brotherhood*.

My indebtedness to an American friend, who prefers to remain anonymous, is very real. Just as real is that to my wife: she has the doubtful privilege of watching my daily uncertainties about matters of English usage turn into relative certainty as I continue to make my slow and complicated way from *a, an* to *-z-, -zz-* in my forthcoming new version of *Modern English Usage*. I am conscious too that some of my most telling illustrative examples come from those submitted to the OED Department quotation files by Mrs Helen Turner and Miss Charlotte Graves Taylor.

R. W. B.

Sutton Courtenay
Oxfordshire
July 1991

Contents

The Fowler Brothers and the Tradition of Usage Handbooks

1. *The tradition of Henry Alford, Richard Grant White, and others*

It is well known that the Fowler brothers, Henry Watson Fowler and Francis George Fowler, wrote *The King's English* (1906, hereafter *TKE*) jointly and that *A Dictionary of Modern English Usage* (1926, hereafter *MEU*) was written by HWF alone[1] because FGF had died in 1918. Throughout their writing lives HWF took the limelight and FGF stood for the most part in the shadows. All the correspondence that the brothers had with the Oxford University Press (hereafter OUP) was in HWF's hand and was signed only by him. Typewritten letters were also signed only by HWF, though until FGF died in 1918 HWF always referred to 'we', not just to himself, when expressing views on particular matters. Such writing partnerships are rare. It just seems to be the case that each article in *TKE* and possibly some of those in *MEU* represent the joint views of the brothers. An examination of the relevant archives held by the OUP[2] revealed no direct evidence of divergence of opinion between the brothers. Nor is it ever made clear which of them wrote the first draft of a particular article or articles. Their upbringing, education, and style of life seem to have

This essay is also published in *English Traditional Grammars: An International Perspective*, ed. Gerhard Leitner (John Benjamins Publishing Co., Amsterdam, 1991).

[1] HWF dedicated *MEU* to his brother: 'to the memory of my brother, Francis George Fowler, M.A. Cantab., who shared with me the planning of this book, but did not live to share the writing . . . The present book . . . contains none of his actual writing; but, having been designed in consultation with him, it is the last fruit of a partnership that began in 1903 with our translation of Lucian.'

[2] I have examined the surviving correspondence between H. W. Fowler and the Oxford University Press from 1909 onwards.

induced in them a seamless or inseparable set of beliefs on all linguistic matters. Or if there were differences of view, they were not allowed to be described outside the cottages that they occupied, only fifty yards apart, on Guernsey.

Both *TKE* and *MEU* are usage manuals written in a tradition mainly inherited from two works of the nineteenth century, one British, Henry Alford's *The Queen's English: Stray notes on speaking and spelling* (1864), and the other American, Richard G. White's *Words and their Uses, Past and Present* (1871). There seems to be no direct reference to Alford in either *TKE* or *MEU*, but HWF mentions him once in a letter to the OUP.[3] There are several quotations from White in *TKE*, e.g. (p. 91):

(The various arrangements of *pueri puellam amabant*) all have the same meaning—the boys loved the girl. For *puellam* shows by its form that it must be the object of the action; *amabant* must have for its subject a plural substantive, and which must therefore be, not *puellam*, but *pueri*.— R. G. White.[4]

The four books differ considerably in length and presentation but the bond that joins them is that each of the authors was attempting to seek out solecisms. This broad aim can be seen in their treatment of the word *mutual*:

What is '*mutual*'? Much the same as '*reciprocal*'. It describes that which passes from each to each of two persons . . . And *mutual* ought never to be used, unless the reciprocity exists. 'The *mutual love* of husband and wife' is correct enough: but 'a *mutual friend* of both husband and wife' is sheer nonsense. (Alford, pp. 205 f.)

. . . *mutual* for *common*, an error not infrequent now even among educated people . . . (White, p. 396)

Every one knows by now that *our mutual friend* is a solecism. *Mutual* implies an action or relation between two or more persons or things, A doing or standing to B as B does or stands to A . . . *Our mutual friend* is nonsense; *mutual friends*, though not nonsense, is bad English, because it is tautological. It takes two to make a friendship, as to make a quarrel; and therefore all friends are mutual friends, and *friends* alone means as much as *mutual friends* . . . (*TKE*, p. 56)

---

[3] 'It [sc. an etymological work proposed by the Fowlers] would be, in a way, on Trench's lines, but not much more like Trench than the King's English is like Alford (Queen's E.)' (letter of 6 Jan. 1911 from HWF to the OUP).

[4] This passage occurs on p. 282 of R. G. White's *Words and their Uses* (3rd edn., 1881).

. . . it follows that *our mutual friend Jones* (meaning Jones who is your friend as well as mine), & all similar phrases, are misuses of *mutual* . . . In such places *common* is the right word, & the use of *mutual* betrays ignorance of its meaning. (*MEU*, pp. 368–9)

It is of interest to observe that, shortly after the publication of *TKE*, the *OED* (in a fascicle published in 1908) presented the 'normal' sense (= 'reciprocal') of *mutual*, with illustrative examples from 1477 onward, and also the 'abnormal' sense (= 'common') with illustrative examples from 1591 onward. In *MEU*, HWF failed to report the history of the two senses, but was content simply to say that 'the *OED*, giving examples of such looseness, goes no further in condemnation than "Now regarded as incorrect", "Commonly censured as incorrect"'. For HWF, *mutual* 'is a well-known trap'. For him, the word has only one permissible meaning.

2. *The planning of* MEU

The early working title of *MEU* was 'an idiom dictionary'. The planning of the work was well under way by 1911:

If you mean by an idiom dictionary what we mean by it, it is so far from having lost favour with us that we are delighted to hear of its surviving in your memory . . . What we mean is a dictionary (or call it a glossary—only the γλῶσσαι are not the out-of-the-way words, but the rest) that should simply not give large classes of words—one-sense words (unless entering into special phrases or with peculiarities of construction or context), scientific & technical words, derivatives (except for limited or peculiar applications), compounds (except when anomalous in sense), & many other sets that would suggest themselves as we got to work.

Space would thus be secured for treating adequately, without making an unwieldy volume, the hard-worked words that form the staple of general talk & writing; their varieties of meaning, liabilities to misuse, difference from synonyms, right & wrong constructions, special collocations, & so forth, could be liberally illustrated, & approval & condemnation less stingily dealt out than has been possible in the official atmosphere of a complete dictionary. The *OED*, by the way, is very chary of pronouncements on the unidiomatic; we irresponsible nobodies should be both more courageous & more directly concerned in the matter. (Handwritten letter of 11 January 1911 from HWF to OUP.)

This plan was judged by the OUP (largely on the advice of Henry Bradley, the lexicographer) to be somewhat too ambitious, and HWF was persuaded to concentrate· on 'liabilities to misuse, difference from synonyms, right & wrong constructions, special collocations, & so forth'. The publishers enthusiastically supported the idea of dealing out approval and condemnation 'less stingily' than was being done in the *OED*.

The formula agreed by OUP and by the Fowlers for the conversion and extension of *TKE* to form a new 'idiom dictionary' was described by Charles Cannan (Secretary to the Delegates of the Clarendon Press) as follows in a letter to HWF dated 13 May 1911:

I myself cannot but think that a companion volume to *The King's English* doing for words alphabetically arranged what that does for words and constructions classified would find a good reception.

The Fowler brothers were content and said that they would embark on such a work and would aim to limit it to 160,000 words in length.

It is important to bear in mind that HWF and FGF did not aim at any readership beyond that of the British Isles:

In point of fact we have our eyes not on the foreigner, but on the half-educated Englishman of literary proclivities who wants to know Can I say so-&-so?, What does this familiar phrase or word mean?, Is this use English?, rather than How do you spell or pronounce so-&-so?, What does this unfamiliar word mean?—the kind of Englishman who has idioms floating in his head in a jumbled state, & knows it . . . Not but what we may be of some use to the foreigner who knows English pretty well; but the foreigner as such we must leave out of consideration. (Typewritten letter from HWF to OUP, 5 April 1911, responding to some criticism of their 'prospectus' for the idiom dictionary by Henry Bradley.)

It is clear from the beginning that the Fowler brothers were not much concerned about the progress of the language in the United States. They seem to have drawn illustrative examples from only four American writers (see below, under 'Sources consulted'). Much later, when it was proposed to publish an American version of *MEU*, HWF wrote to the OUP as follows:

To begin with, I have not the least objection to *MEU*'s being americanized to any desired extent, provided it is just made clear that I have no responsibility for the changes. I should not be able to help at all, because I know absolutely nothing about American; but I don't gather that you would mind my taking no part. (HWF to Kenneth Sisam, OUP, 17 July 1927.)

HWF went on to emphasize that much of the value of *MEU* lay in its British examples:

To the English reader they are obviously genuine because he sees their like in his newspaper every day, & can usually even guess their context; but the 100% American (as opposed to the 50/50 Anglo-American who is well content with *MEU* as it is) does not see quite the same sort of writing, half the things mentioned in the quotations are unfamiliar to him, & he will find himself in an alien atmosphere. Moreover, lots of things are laboriously argued out that are for Americans not living issues but *choses jugées*, & others that excite Americans are ignored. (Ibid.)

3. *The relationship between* TKE *and* MEU

Since both works are usage manuals there is a great deal of overlap in subject matter. But there the resemblance ends. *TKE* is arranged in topics, whereas *MEU* is arranged alphabetically in the manner of a dictionary. *TKE* is only half the length of *MEU*. *TKE* cites the names of the authors, newspapers, etc., from which the illustrative examples are drawn (just the names, with no titles of books, no chapter or page numbers, no dates), whereas virtually all of *MEU*'s examples are unattributed. *MEU*'s illustrative examples seem hardly ever to be the same as those in *TKE*.[5]

Though the topics treated overlap, the entries in *MEU*, i.e. the later work, are always rewritten. Compare, for example, the treatment of the expression *leading question* in the two books:

TKE, p. 306: Before *leading question* or *the exception proves the rule* is written, a lawyer should be consulted . . . A leading question is one that unfairly helps a witness to the desired answer. [Long illustrative example from *The Times*.]

MEU, p. 318: *leading question* is often misused for a poser—or a pointed question or one that goes to the heart of the matter (as though *leading* meant principal); its real meaning is quite different; a l. q. is not hostile, but friendly, & is so phrased as to guide or lead the person questioned to the answer that it is desirable for him to make, but that he might not think of making or be able to make without help . . . [No illustrative example.]

Comparison of other entries (e.g. *lay* and *lie*, *like* as a conjunction, *literary critics' words*, *Malaprops*, *oblivious to/of*, and so on, shows that the verdicts and attitudes presented in the two works were essentially the same, but that in every case the later articles

[5] A rare exception occurs in comments on the word *legislature* in the two books. *TKE* cites an example from the works of (John) Morley. *MEU* gives the same illustrative example (unattributed), but the wording of the comments is different in the two books.

have been rewritten and expanded, and the arguments have been supported by fresh illustrative examples.

4. *Sources consulted by the Fowlers*

A profile of the newspapers, periodicals, and books that HWF and FGF consulted in the three-year period 1903–6 can be built up from an analysis of the works most frequently cited in the text of *TKE*. Of newspapers and periodicals, *The Times* supplied the most examples by far (some 550), followed by the *Daily Telegraph* (96) and the *Spectator* (74). The two local papers in Guernsey, the *Guernsey Advertiser* and the *Guernsey Evening Press*, are cited occasionally, and there are isolated examples from other journalistic sources, including one each from the *Cheltenham Examiner*, the *Daily Express*, *Tit-bits*, and the *Lamp*. Learned journals are nowhere cited.

The authors drawn on included a select group of eighteenth-century writers (Burke, Fanny Burney, Cowper, Goldsmith, Johnson, Richardson, Smollett, Sterne, and Swift), and a much larger contingent of nineteenth-century ones (Bagehot, Beaconsfield, E. F. Benson, Borrow, C. Brontë, Hall Caine, Carlyle, De Quincey, Dickens, A. Conan Doyle, George Eliot, Galt, Gladstone, Hazlitt, Jowett, Lamb, Landor, Macaulay, Meredith, John Morley, Thomas Love Peacock, Ruskin, Walter Scott, Herbert Spencer, Leslie Stephen, R. L. Stevenson, Thackeray, Trollope, H. G. Wells, Wilde, and (once only) W. B. Yeats). Less well-known authors whose works are cited from relatively often are Marie Corelli (a prolific popular writer), Francis Marion Crawford (ditto), S. R. Crockett (of the Scottish 'Kailyard School' of writers), Susan Ferrier (author of several Scottish novels published in the early nineteenth century), John R. Green (historian), William H. Prescott (American historian), and Douglas B. W. Sladen (who edited some Australian poetry and wrote about Japan).

The American writers whose works were drawn on are a very select few: Emerson, Henry James, J. R. Lowell, and Poe.

No account survives of the actual manner in which the Fowlers excerpted and filed the illustrative examples that they used in *TKE*.

It looks as if their personal library was a small one, and the sources drawn on would hardly be considered to be a satisfactory sampling by present-day standards. Scores of important writers of the Victorian period remained unexamined, or, at any rate, uncited, writers like Ainsworth, Louisa M. Alcott, Matthew Arnold, Bulwer Lytton, Mrs Gaskell, Charles Kingsley, John Stuart Mill, and so on.

A sampling of the illustrative examples indicates, rather surprisingly perhaps, that the Fowlers very rarely drew them from the *OED*. Thus in *TKE*, for example, in paragraph 1 on pp. 4–5, the pattern is as follows:

brisken, v. (E. F. Benson): the word is given in *OED* with a citation from Benson but not the one in *TKE*.

deplacement (*The Times*): the word is not in *OED*.

insuccess (*The Times*): in *OED* but the *TKE* example is a fresh one.

remindful (Meredith): same example in *OED* and *TKE* but as the relevant fascicle of *OED* was published only in January 1906 it is likely that the Fowlers obtained the example independently.

Comparison of other sections of *TKE* with the *OED* confirmed that the Fowler brothers assembled their own independent evidence in virtually every case throughout the book.[6]

Their dependence on other works is described explicitly only in one section of *TKE*, the long section on punctuation. Thus:

to those readers who would prefer a careful, systematic, and not over-long treatise, Beadnell's *Spelling and Punctuation* (Wyman, 2/6) is recommended. (*TKE*, p. 219)

This is Henry Beadnell's *Spelling and Punctuation: A Manual for Authors, Students, and Printers*, first published, it would appear,[7] at some point in the 1880s.

Another work mentioned in the same chapter (p. 237) is Allen G. Bigelow's *Manual of Punctuation*.[8]

Many of the problems identified in this world of commas, dashes, colons, and so on, are now arcane:

It must be added, however, that Beadnell himself helps to make things worse, by countenancing the strange printer's superstition that (,—) is beautiful to look upon, and (—,) ugly. (*TKE*, p. 266)

---

[6] One should bear in mind that the *OED* had not got beyond the early part of the letter *R* by 1906.

[7] In the National Union Catalogue the sixth edition is listed as xii, 178 p., 188–?, London: E. Menken, and a later edition as xii, 178 p., 1919, London: Myers & Co. There seem to be no copies of any edition in the Bodleian Library or the British Library.

[8] This is Allen Gilman Bigelow.

or highly personal to the Fowlers:

First comes what may be called for short the spot-plague—the tendency to make full-stops do all the work. (*TKE*, p. 226)

HWF's own punctuation is marked by two very characteristic features—an over-use of the semi-colon (in place of the full stop) and (in *MEU*) the use of the ampersand (&) throughout the book both in the editorial comments and in the illustrative examples.

In *TKE* (pp. 311, 343), the Fowlers also drew illustrative examples from two contemporary usage guides by John Bygott and A. J. Lawford Jones. One of these actually bore the title *The King's English and How to Write It* (London, 1904). It was, as its subtitle says,

A Comprehensive Text-Book of Essay Writing, Précis Writing, and Paraphrasing, with Hints for a Practical and Representative Course of Reading. Intended for every English-speaking person who would learn to write correctly and gracefully, and adapted to the needs of Candidates for all Civil Service, University, Board of Education, and other Examinations demanding a knowledge of English Composition.

The other book by these two authors dealt with matters of punctuation. It was *Points in Punctuation; or, How to punctuate the King's English* (London, date of first edition not known, second edition 1905).

5. *Assessments of the value of* MEU

The fact that both *TKE* and *MEU* are still (1989) in print in lightly revised editions suggests that both works have retained their general appeal. It is of interest, therefore, to observe the sharp divergence of opinion about the value of the first edition of *MEU* (1926), as shown in reviews of the book that appeared soon after it was published.

Hilda M. R. Murray, in *The Year's Work in English Studies 1926*, pointed the way to the allure of *MEU*:

Of books to delight the general reader and kindle his interest in linguistic studies Mr. Fowler's *Dictionary of Modern English Usage* is one of the most alluring. It combines the function of a guide to the correct use of the language with that of a literary encyclopaedia, and may still be successful in checking the all too rapid advance of illiteracies, such as *alright*, among the nominally educated. The plan and execution are alike admirable and the matter excellent reading, though the reader may sometimes fail to distinguish between the voice of authority and that of private opinion.

Frank Sidgwick reviewed it for *The Review of English Studies* (1926, pp. 490–2) and emphasized the tendency for the book to induce self-consciousness in a person's own writing.

May he [sc. the reviewer] call the book a farrago? Or is that word black-listed under PEDANTRY, HACKNEYED PHRASES, or ELEGANT VARIATION? No, apparently not; nor under LITERARY WORDS, nor (he sighs with relief) under LITERARY CRITICS' WORDS. Is it then permissible on other grounds?—for the Dictionary stimulates its owner to extreme self-consciousness.

Ernest Weekley in *The London Mercury* (1926, pp. 667–8) welcomed the book but did not believe that it would stem the tide of misuse in English newspapers:

For years Mr. Fowler has been taking notes. He has watched the increasing stream that passes from the Press and he has seen that it is not only bad, but that it is steadily getting worse. I hardly think he can have much hope that his book will dam or purify it. Those who know and respect the English language will study him with interest and perhaps cure themselves of a few unseemly tricks and habits, but the dwellers in the wilderness, the regular sinners against all canons of grammar, clarity and taste, will either stop their ears or regard him as a setter-forth of strange gods.

George T. Flom said in the *Journal of English and Germanic Philology* (1928, pp. 142–3) that he believed that the 'book should have a distinct influence for good'. 'The young writer will find this dictionary a mine of information and sound advice; and the general student of English will use it with profit.' But he went on to criticize HWF's lack of mastery of phonetics:

The special student of the English language will at once be exasperated over the phonetic notation employed, the unscientific terminology used in explaining sounds, and the incorrect use of English words in these explanations ('the harder *ch*' of Scotch, etc., as compared with the *sh* of Welsh, p. 704; '*g* is reckoned hard (get), *s* is reckoned hard (set),' p. 436 . . .).

Kemp Malone in *Modern Language Notes* (1927, pp. 201–2) sees much to praise:

He [sc. HWF] reveals himself . . . as master of his material and delightful in its presentation. The book is eminently readable. It swarms with 'general articles' having seductive titles like *Cannibalism, Malaprops, Superiority, Unequal Yokefellows*, etc.

But he then turns on Fowler:

Yet nowadays we make great demands on an author of an authoritative work on any subject. It is not enough that he have his material well in hand and agreeably set forth. We expect him to be trained in scientific method, and dominated by the scientific point of view. Now in Mr. Fowler's chosen field of activity, viz. linguistic science, sound and abiding work cannot be done by a man weak in phonetics and neglectful of the historical approach to the problems of which he writes. And Mr. Fowler, unfortunately enough, cannot well be denied both weakness in phonetics and neglect of history.

MEU is sharply dismissed as 'a collection of linguistic prejudices presented by a clever advocate'.

The most severe criticism, however, came from continental scholars. The Dutch scholar, P. Fijn van Draat (in *Englische Studien*, 1928, pp. 82–6) recognized the value of Fowler's articles on various topics:

A fine touch, wide reading, felicitous wording combine to give us a collection of synonyms such as we look for in vain elsewhere. Fowler's articles on *large, big and great*; on *small and little*; on *act and action*—to mention only a few—are simply superb.

But he found many faults. Pruning of many articles was desirable, he thought ('the author has forgotten that brevity is the soul of wit'). He questioned Fowler's claim (p. 616) 'that in Latin *s* between two vowels becomes *r*. In reality it is *z* that undergoes the change; *s* never becomes *r*.' Above all he attacks the 'grammar part' of the book as 'altogether unsatisfactory'.

He speaks of the place of the adverb and does not know Western's meritorious essay. In his treatment of such words as *quite, right, full, very*, etc. Stoffel's exhaustive studies are totally ignored, just as Poutsma's work is overlooked, where the author discusses the *Gerund, Hendiadys, need* and *dare*. He has no idea of the important issues he raises when discussing the question of the consonant in *elfish* or *elvish*, because he has never read Jespersen's *Studier over Engelske kasus*, nor, for that matter, any other work of the same scholar; else the articles 'Cognate object,' 'Hyphens' and others would have worn a different aspect. Of spelling-pronunciation Fowler has never heard. His long article on the Split Infinitive is in the old vein: that Rhythm may have something to do with it, he does not even suspect.

Another scathing attack was mounted by the Dutch Anglicist and grammarian Etsko Kruisinga (in *English Studies*, 1928, pp. 181–5):

it is certain that the writer of a good dictionary is often not a good grammarian, or even not a grammarian at all. Mr. Fowler, unfortunately, is no exception; to him a grammarian may be all sorts of things but never what he ought to be in our opinion: a student of language.

He presents Fowler in various roles: the Grammarian as Moralist (because he says that the perfect infinitive ought to be used only to express past time); the Grammarian as Policeman (because Fowler in his article on Cases says 'if novelists are to be trusted'); the Grammarian as a Judge of Style (because in the article on the Double Passive he fails to see that passive constructions involving different kinds of verbs will naturally operate differently); and the Grammarian as Conjuror (because of his deficient treatment of the indefinite article before 'silent *h*' and of relative pronouns). His main point, however, is unsound: 'Oxford people . . . should avoid one thing: they should not set up as guides to foreigners, as they do in this work, which is evidently meant for foreign consumption too.'

I have already made it clear that Fowler's aims were entirely insular. And Kruisinga's equation of Fowler with Oxford seems to imply that he believed Fowler to be an Oxford don. His attack is seriously wide of the mark.

It would appear that the general public and scholars other than professional linguists were ready to heap praise on the vigorous arguments about disputed points of usage set forth in *MEU*, and for the most part were ready to accept Fowler's judgements. Professional linguistic scholars, on the other hand, had no difficulty in locating and condemning weaknesses in Fowler's knowledge of many of the complexities of modern English grammar, and especially his unscientific treatment of phonetics.

6. *Assessments of the second edition (1965) of* MEU

Sir Ernest Gowers, who prepared the second edition of *MEU*, admitted that he was 'chary of making any substantial alterations except for the purpose of bringing him [sc. Fowler] up to date'.[9] Inevitably the publication of the new edition elicited the same sharp division of opinion as that of 1926. An anonymous reviewer

---

[9] p. ix of Gowers' second edition of *MEU* (1965).

in *British Book News* July 1965 expressed the traditional favourable view:

Sir Ernest Gowers' greatest achievement is his preservation of the unique Fowleresque quality which has made the book perennial and gives pleasure with enlightenment to all its discerning users.

Similarly an anonymous reviewer in the *Teachers' World* (12 November 1965) said that 'Mention of the names of Defenders of English must bring me to Fowler, whose *Modern English Usage* made him the greatest champion and paladin of them all'. The reviewer attacked 'some pressmen and most ad-men' and especially 'the TV ad-men' because 'they seek to knock the guts out of English and rob it of meaning. They are the underminers.' For the reviewer, Fowler was 'the pope of English usage . . . the infallible and sole arbiter'.

Anthony Burgess reviewed the edition in the *Observer* (9 May 1965) under the heading 'Switched-on Fowler'; better informed than most people about the difference between linguistic descriptivism and prescriptivism, he commented acidly:

Nowadays we question self-appointed authority, and rightly. Who is Fowler to tell us what to say? We expect a dictionary of usage to describe what people do, not what they ought to do, and the scientific linguists (Fowler was not one of those; he was a schoolmaster) unite in reminding us that no one, not even the Newspeak commissars, can legislate for language.

A scientific linguist of great distinction, Barbara M. H. Strang, did not hold back in her article for *Modern Language Review* (1966, pp. 264–5): 'Fowler's attitude is not a possible one for a good mind in the 1960s, and the attempt at modernization leads Gowers into irreconcileable conflicts.' She then lists numerous examples of 'irreconcileable conflicts', including 'snide remarks about literary critics' and writing which 'shows a diffuseness or lack of edge, sometimes a want of the courage of the author's convictions or an inconclusive petulance, that are not at all Fowlerian (cf. *Abstractitis, Aggravate, Atom, Dedicated, Finalize, Flamboyant*)'.

Perhaps the most severe assessment of *MEU*, however, had appeared in 1958, the centenary of HWF's birth. In the *Listener* (13 March 1958), Randolph Quirk, after giving all due praise to Fowler's lexicographical skill, went on to attack his competence as a grammarian and linguist. It is van Draat and Kruisinga over again:

he was no great grammarian, still less a linguist in the modern scientific sense . . . Any of a score of his major articles on grammar shows clearly his deficiencies in this field.

Quirk points to Fowler's inconsistencies:

He feels strongly enough to describe 'it's me' as a blunder in one place, though elsewhere with rather more sense of proportion he lets it pass as 'a lapse of no importance' . . . While he deprecates on one page the *s* genitive in usages like 'the narrative's charm', he falls into the practice himself elsewhere with 'the termination's possibilities' and 'the sentence's structure'.

In particular he scorns Fowler's riposte (*SPE Tract* xxvi, 1927, pp. 192–6) to the strictures of Otto Jespersen (*SPE Tract* xxv, 1926, pp. 147–72), especially HWF's insistence on the close relationship between Latin and English grammar. Fowler insisted (ibid. 194–5):

Professor Jespersen probably knows more Latin grammar than I do, but he would have it kept severely to its own language. I cannot agree. Whether or not it is regrettable that we English have for centuries been taught what little grammar we know on Latin traditions, have we not now to recognize that the iron has entered into our souls, that our grammatical conscience has by this time a Latin element inextricably compounded in it, if not predominant . . .

No resolution of such arguments is possible. There is no doubt that members of the general public and academic scholars who are not linguistic scientists still put their faith in usage guides, partly because of the complexity of many modern descriptive grammars of English, and partly because of a persistent though erroneous belief (whatever scholars like Jespersen say) that Latin grammar has some kind of causal hold on English grammar.

7. *Modern usage guides*

It is impossible here to do much more than list some of the most important usage guides of the period since 1926. Perhaps the best known are as follows (listed in chronological order):

Eric Partridge, *Usage and Abusage. A Guide to Good English*, 1942
Bergen Evans and Cornelia Evans, *A Dictionary of Contemporary American Usage*, 1957
G. Porter Perrin, *Writer's Guide and Index to English*, 1959
Wilson Follett, *Modern American Usage*. Completed by Jacques Barzun, 1966.

William Morris and Mary Morris, *Harper Dictionary of Contemporary Usage*, 1975.

Sidney Greenbaum and Janet Whitcut, *Longman Guide to English Usage*, 1988.

Webster's Dictionary of English Usage, 1989

It is a simple matter to show that there is no consensus in the choice of headwords in the main usage manuals and in the extent of their treatment. Cf. ten consecutive headwords in four of the manuals and the varying amount of space given to the entries for these headwords:

MEU 1926	Partridge 1942	Longman 1988	Webster 1989
if & when	if and when	if	if and when
ignite	if as how	ignoramus	if worst comes to worst
ignoramus	if need be	-ile	ignoramus
ignoratio elenchi	if not	ilex	I guess
ignore	-ify	ilk	ilk
ilex	ignoramus	ill, sick	ill
ilk	ignorant	illegal,	illegible, un-
illegible, unreadable	-ile and -ine	illegitimate, illicit	readable illicit
illiteracies	ilk, of that	illegible, unreadable	illogical comparison
illogicalities	ill and sick	illicit	illusion
Total: 3⅓ pages	1½ pages	2 pages	2 pages

MEU 1926 has 4 pages on *metaphor*, Partridge 1942 5¾ pages, Longman 1988 ¾ page, and there is no entry for the word in Webster 1989. The respective entries for *split infinitive* occupy 2 pages in *MEU* 1926, ½ page in Partridge 1942 and in Longman 1988, and 1½ pages in Webster 1989. *MEU* 1926 has an entry for *position of adverbs* that runs to 4¾ pages; Partridge 1942 has nearly 2 pages on the matter under the heading *order of words*; Longman 1988 has a short article under *adverbs, position of*; Webster 1989 discusses the subject briefly under adverbs. Longman 1988 is the only one of the four to comment on the position of the main stress in *controversy* and *formidable*, at least as separate articles. *Hopefully* in its now common use as a sentence adverb hardly existed when *MEU* 1926 and Partridge 1942 were written; both Longman 1988 and Webster 1989 make observations about its acceptability. *MEU* 1926 and Partridge 1942 condemn the use of *meticulous* in the sense 'scrupulous about minute details'; Longman 1988 and Webster 1989, by contrast, regard the older sense '*over-scrupulous about minute details*' as now effectively obsolete. Partridge 1942 included (pp. 59–83) a long list of clichés. *MEU* 1926 had a long entry (pp. 597–627) for the TECHNICAL TERMS of rhetoric, grammar, logic, prosody, diplomacy, literature, etc. None of the other usage guides saw the merit of entries for such items (*acatalectic, ad captandum, alcaics, anacrusis, anastrophe, aposiopesis*, etc.).

TKE had many entries under idiosyncratic headwords: e.g. ANTICS; BETWEEN TWO STOOLS; BRACHYLOGY; CLUMSY PATCHING; FAR-FETCHED WORDS; SPOT-PLAGUE; UNEQUAL YOKEFELLOWS; and WENS AND HYPERTROPHIED MEMBERS. Fowler introduced equally opaque headwords in *MEU* 1926: e.g. BATTERED ORNAMENTS, CANNIBALISM, ELEGANT VARIATION, LEGERDEMAIN WITH TWO SENSES, OUT OF THE FRYING-PAN, PAIRS & SNARES, STURDY INDEFENSIBLES, and SWAPPING HORSES. The Fowler brothers clearly expected their readers to get to 'know' the books well enough to realize what kind of information was likely to be found under them. The other usage guides keep fairly strictly to traditional language in their headwords.

TKE and *MEU* were based on the assumption that national newspapers and a limited range of well-known writers were suitable and sufficient quarries for the preparation of guides to English usage. By contrast, Webster 1989 bases its recommend-ations on an immense file of linguistic evidence in the Merriam–Webster quotation files. Morris 1975 depends substantially on the judgements made by members of a usage panel. Future guides will inevitably be dependent on evidence held in large computer databases. Such varied approaches are natural and healthy in a world where (*a*) technology is developing apace, (*b*) local variation of usage is increasing in all the main English-speaking areas, (*c*) where prescriptive and descriptive attitudes stand in opposition to each other.

Uncancellable attitudes, not always very logically expressed, towards present-day English usage continue to be a feature of everyday life. In the course of a single day at three separate social occasions in Oxford in early June 1989, two of them garden parties for academic members of the University of Oxford and the third a dinner party, I noted down the various points of usage that 'worried' the guests I met. Readers of the present article will not be surprised to hear that they were *between you and I* (and similar pronominal constructions), *different from/to/than*, *lay/lie*, *may/ might*, *shall/will*, and split infinitives. I mentioned that these points of usage had been in dispute since at least the time of Henry Alford's *The Queen's English* (1864). No one was particularly impressed nor showed that their 'worry' was therefore in any way diminished. Obviously many things have happened in the world in the last century and a quarter, but such a period is a very short time indeed in the slowly turning axis of attitudes towards 'correct' English usage.[10]

[10] Further information on the Fowlers may be found in: George G. Coulton's essay, 'H. W. Fowler', *SPE Tract* XLIII, 1935. Robert Burchfield's lecture for the English Association, 'The Fowlers, their Achievements in Lexicography and Grammar' (1979), reprinted in *Unlocking the English Language*, by Robert Burchfield, pp. 125–46, 1989.

2

An Outline History of Euphemisms in English

1. Definitions

With the exception of the period before the Norman Conquest, when the evidence is too sparse to reach any reasonable conclusions, all periods of English can be seen to have been characterized by the presence of explicit or neutral vocabulary side by side with synonyms or near-synonyms of varying degrees of inexplicitness. The synonyms that are 'well-sounding' are often but not always euphemisms.

Euphemism is defined in dictionaries as a rhetorical device: 'substitution of mild or vague or roundabout expression for harsh or blunt or direct one' (*Concise Oxford Dictionary*, 7th edition, 1982). It also has a concrete meaning: 'a polite, tactful, or less explicit term used to avoid the direct naming of an unpleasant, painful, or frightening reality' (*Webster's Third New International Dictionary*, 1961). The word *euphemism* is first recorded in English in Thomas Blount's *Glossographia* (1656), where it is defined as 'a good or favourable interpretation of a bad word'. It is derived from the Greek words ευφημισμός 'use of an auspicious word for an inauspicious one' and εύφημος 'fair of speech'. The employment of euphemisms can be viewed positively as the use of words of good omen, or negatively as the avoidance of unlucky or inauspicious words. Curiously Dr Johnson excluded the word from his *Dictionary of the English Language* (1755) though it had appeared in his main source, Nathan Bailey's *Dictionarium Britannicum* (1730), stressed on the second syllable, and defined as 'good name, reputation, an honourable setting forth one's praise'.

Standard reference works cite *intimacy* as a euphemism for *sexual intercourse, pass away* for *die, underprivileged* for *poor*, and

First published in *Fair of Speech: The Uses of Euphemism*, edited by D. J. Enright (Oxford University Press, 1985), 13–31.

made redundant for *dismissed*. Older writers tend to cite some-what more literary examples, for example *a shorn crown* for *decapitation* and *gentleman of the road* for a *highwayman*.

Dr Thomas Bowdler in his edition of Shakespeare (10 volumes, 1818) removed from Shakespeare's text 'those words and expressions . . . which cannot with propriety be read aloud in a family'. He sometimes did this by substituting innocuous words for unacceptable ones. Thus in *Antony and Cleopatra*, I. i. 10, 'a gipsy's lust' became in Bowdler's version 'a gipsy's will'; in *Othello*, v. i. 36, 'Thy bed, lust-stain'd, shall with lust's blood be spotted' became 'Thy bed, now stain'd, shall with thy blood be spotted'; and in *Hamlet*, v. ii. 64, 'He that hath kill'd my king and whor'd my mother' became 'He that hath kill'd my king seduc'd my mother'. Elsewhere passages were simply removed from the text. Thus 'Royal wench! She made great Cæsar lay his sword to bed. He ploughed her, and she cropp'd' (*Antony and Cleopatra*, II. ii. 230–2) appeared in Bowdler's text only as 'Royal wench! She made great Cæsar lay his sword to bed'. Families needed to be protected from the sexual innuendo of ploughing and cropping.

In the second half of the present century attitudes towards sexual behaviour have changed considerably. The generative organs and their conjunctions have been stripped of immodesty. Instead a marked tendency has emerged to place screens of euphemism round the terminology of politics and race. Key words include *peace, democracy, human rights, freedom, the troubles, emergency, intervention, invasion, campaign*, and *rescue mission*; and *Black*, instead of *Negro, darky, savage, coon*, etc. *Freedom fighters* or *partisans* are seen by their opponents as *terrorists*. Political killers *claim*, or alternatively *admit*, responsibility for assassinating/murdering/killing other people. The terminology arises from the passionate ideological battles of our age. At less bellicose levels, the aged tend to be called *senior citizens*, backward children are said to be *mentally handicapped* or *educationally subnormal*, and juvenile law-breakers are sent to *approved schools*. Bookmakers tend now to call themselves *turf accountants*, and undertakers have become *funeral directors*.

2. *Contextual difficulties*

It is impossible at present to write a definitive history of euphemisms. One major impediment is the alphabetical arrangement of dictionaries: no work exists in which all the synonyms of a given period of the past can be unscrambled and set side by side. Another lies in the area of contextual interpretation. In 'The deep damnation of his taking-off' (*Macbeth*, I. vii. 20) *taking-off* is sometimes taken to be a euphemism for 'murder'. But Shakespeare does not abjure the word *murder* or its explicit synonyms elsewhere: indeed the word *murderer* actually occurs in the same famous speech ('If it were done when 'tis done . . .'). *Taking-off* is simply a poetical variant in its context, not a true euphemism. Shakespeare is no tender-hearted precursor of Thomas Bowdler.

A further difficulty lies in the interpretation of the complex social arrangements and attitudes of periods before one's own lifetime. It is never easy and often impossible to recognize the true nature of fine distinctions of meaning in the works of writers of the past. In Dryden's *Marriage à la Mode* (1673), a comedy concerned with affairs of love, the words *intrigue* and *amour* are contrasted:

PHILOTIS: 'Tis great pity Rhodophil's a married man, that you may not have an honorable intrigue with him.

MELANTHA: Intrigue, Philotis! That's an old phrase; I have laid that word by: *amour* sounds better.   (II. ii)

But *intrigue* is now an even older and altogether more archaic word. Allowance needs to be made for the semantic erosions of time.

The language of adversaries has always been just as selectively self-directing as it is at the present time but the subject-matter in the past was often very different. Thus Shylock's *well-worn thrift* is called *interest* by Antonio: the adversarial language (from Shylock's point of view) arises because Antonio 'hates our sacred nation' and 'in low simplicity . . . lends out money gratis'.

Euphemisms of the past are of course often clearly distinguishable and no more so than in some works of the Victorian period. A good many of Dickens's characters display impressive dexterity in avoiding the use of the names of certain articles of dress:

Mr Trotter . . . gave four distinct slaps on the pocket of his mulberry indescribables . . .   (*The Pickwick Papers*, ch. XVI)

Other nineteenth-century authors show the same reluctance to employ the word *trousers* or *breeches*:

A fine lady can talk about her lover's inexpressibles, when she would faint to hear of his breeches.   (*OED*, 1809)

The priest's unmentionables drying on a hedge.   (*OED*, 1883)

In practice, however, trousers and underclothes were doubtless ordered or purchased by name, however 'faint' fine ladies were said to feel when mention was made of them. It was just that it was genteel to assume that there were holes in the language, invisible words, expressions that should be reserved for day-to-day mercantile business but were deemed unsuitable for use in polite circles.

3. *Scholarly assumptions*

For linguistic scholars a standard example of the ritual avoidance of an inauspicious word lies in the fate of the reconstructed primitive Indo-European word for *bear*, namely *ṛksos*. It survives in Sanskrit (*ṛkšas*), Greek (*ἄρκτος*), and Latin (*ursus*), but has disappeared in language areas where the bear was at one time an object of terror, that is in Germanic and Slavonic languages. In the Balto-Slavonic group of languages it has been replaced by the types represented by Russian *medved'*, 'honey-eater' and Lithuanian *lokys*, 'licker'. In the Germanic languages (Old English *bera*, Modern English *bear*, German *Bär*, Dutch *beer*, etc.) it has been replaced by derivatives of the Indo-European noun meaning 'the brown one'.

Another standard example of the avoidance of an ill-omened word is the presence in Old English of the words *swefan, sweltan,* and *steorfan*, all meaning 'to die', but originally or also meaning 'to sleep', 'to burn slowly', and 'to grow stiff' respectively. The unrecorded verb *degan*, cognate with Old Norse *deyja*, almost certainly existed in Old English, as the verb corresponding to *dēaþ*, 'death' and *dēad*, 'dead', but it was avoided in writing until the taboo on it was lifted by some releasing mechanism soon after the Norman Conquest.

Jonathan Swift says of the Houyhnhnms (*Gulliver's Travels*, 1726) that 'they have no word in their language to express anything that is evil'. By 'evil' he means such things as 'the folly of a servant, an omission of a child, a stone that cut their feet, a continuance of foul or unseasonable weather, or the like'. But among the unmentionables is death. He relates a story of a Houyhnhnm who made an appointment with a friend and his family to come to his house upon some affair of importance:

On the day fixed the mistress and her two children came very late; she made two excuses, first for her husband, who, as she said, happened that very morning to 'shnuwnh'. The word is strongly expressive in their language, but not easily rendered into English; it signifies, to retire to his first mother.

Her husband had in fact died, and the Houyhnhnm wife, like the Anglo-Saxons, was using her own euphemism for 'to die'.

4. *Substitutions*

One way to sidestep explicitness is to use a range of substitute symbols like asterisks or dashes or to use abbreviations or other semi-concealing devices. In *Tristram Shandy* (1759–67) Laurence Sterne provides a classic example of asterisks replacing an explicit sexual word:

My sister, I dare say, added he, does not care to let a man come so near her ****. I will not say whether my uncle Toby had completed the sentence or not;—'tis for his advantage to suppose he had,—as, I think, he could have added no One Word which would have improved it.

The missing word, contextually, is *pudenda* or equivalent. Sterne teases us by pretending that it is an example of aposiopesis:

Take the dash away, and write Backside,—'tis Bawdy.—Scratch Backside out, and put Covered way in, 'tis a Metaphor; and, I dare say, as fortification ran so much in my uncle Toby's head, that if he had been left to have added one word to the sentence,—that word was it.

The actual conception of Tristram Shandy is also euphemistically presented as a 'little family concernment' between his father and mother, associated with the regular winding of a large house-clock 'on the first Sunday-night of every month':

He had likewise gradually brought some other little family concernments to the same period, in order . . . to get them all out of the way at one time, and be no more plagued and pestered with them the rest of the month.

Other types of euphemistic substitution are very common. Moll Flanders does not have large breasts, but is 'well-carriaged'. She describes her first near-seduction in the following manner:

However, though he took these freedoms with me, it did not go to that, which they call the last favour, which, to do him justice, he did not attempt . . .

And when she eventually succumbs to her first seducer:

> I made no more resistance to him, but let him do just what he pleased, and as often as he pleased.

Inauspicious words and unlucky actions are thus skilfully screened by lightly imaginative language.

Henry Fielding softens the barbarousness of the gallows by describing Jonathan Wild's execution 'on the tree of glory' as only 'a dance without music':

> This was the day of the execution, or consummation, or apotheosis (for it is called by different names), which was to give our hero an opportunity of facing death and damnation, without any fear in his heart.

Damnation, in more Christian ages than ours, was an ultimate obscenity. So too, more trivially, were and are interjections like *damn*, *Christ*, *Jesus*, and saints' names (*by St ——*). The evasions are of several kinds:

> He even went so far as to D   Mr Baps to Lady Skettles . . .
> (Charles Dickens, *Dombey and Son*, ch. 14)

> Though 'bother it' I may
> Occasionally say,
> I never use a big, big, D—.
> (W. S. Gilbert, *HMS Pinafore*, 1)

> Geeze, was that you? What were you doing up there?
> (David Lodge, *The British Museum is Falling Down*, ch. 10)

> 'Jeepers Creepers!' he said to himself, remembering the expression on Mr Stoyte's face.
> (Aldous Huxley, *After Many a Summer*, part II, ch. 9).

> For Chrissake, grow up.
> (J. D. Salinger, *Catcher in the Rye*, ch. 3)

> Jiminy Christmas! That gives me the blue creevies.
> (Rudyard Kipling, *Captains Courageous*, ch. 4)

> That's what it was—oh, cripes!—awful hole.
> (J. B. Priestley, *Angel Pavement*, ch. 4)

Rhyming slang is another semi-concealing device: *bristols*, 'breasts' (from *Bristol cities* = *titties*), *cobblers*, 'nonsense, balls' (from *cobbler's awls* = *balls*), and *Hampton Wick*, 'penis' (rhyming with *prick*). Concealment is also partially achieved by abbreviations and by acronyms: *sweet FA* = (politely) *sweet Fanny Adams*, 'nothing at all', (impolitely) *sweet fuck all*; *snafu* = (politely) *situation normal all fouled up*, (impolitely) *situation normal all fucked up*.

A euphemistic device of an altogether different kind is employed by Thomas Rowlandson (1756–1827). He depicted the brutal and libidinous side of the days of George III and the Regency in a series of erotic paintings with stunningly punning captions like 'The Finishing Stroke' (showing a cuckolded husband about to fire a blunderbuss at his wife's lover caught *in flagrante delicto*), and 'The Country Squire New Mounted' (showing a lecherous squire achieving sexual union while mounted on a horse). Even the notorious libertine, the Earl of Rochester (1648–80), whose usual style lacks disguise of any kind,

> Much wine had past with grave discourse
> Of who Fucks who, and who does worse,

sometimes resorts to euphemistic circumlocutions for parts of the anatomy:

> By swift degrees, advancing where
> His daring Hand that Altar seiz'd,
> Where Gods of Love, do Sacrifice!
> That awful Throne! that Paradise!

5. *Anglo-Saxon attitudes*

In its earliest form English, like the early forms of many other languages, seems like a restricted, almost a censored, secretion, recorded only in its best regulated form. It is almost as if its main reason for surviving was to supply paradigms and fine-spun sentences for grammarians and literary historians. It is almost certainly right to assume however that the *speech* of our forebears in the Anglo-Saxon period, however hedged about by rules and customs, was, as now, untidy, approximate, illogical, and also (when necessary) euphemistic.

However true this general proposition is, one looks more or less in vain for undisputed euphemisms in the central corpus of Old English literary prose and verse. *Sceandword* (opprobrious words) certainly existed, but in medical works and ancient glossaries, not in works like *Beowulf* or the elevated prose of the period.

The vocabulary of the latrine or privy, for example, can be ascertained from Anglo-Saxon works like the *Leechdoms*. Most of the recorded synonyms are based on the notion of 'going' or 'sitting' or of the resemblance of the latrine to a pit or a ditch. The most usual word seems to have been *gang* or *gong* (*OED Gong*[1]), a special use of the same word (*OED Gang* sb.[1]) meaning 'a journeying, a going; eventually, a set of persons, a gang'. Obvious extensions of it occur in *earsgang* (arse-privy, scarcely euphemistic!), *forðgang*, and *ūtgang*; and, with added second elements, *gang-ærn* (*ærn* place), *-pytt* (pit), *-setl* (seat), *-stōl* (stool, seat), and *-tūn* (separate building). The other main synonyms are abundantly transparent: *ādel(a)* (filthy place), *feltūn* (field building), and *grēp(e)* (ditch, drain).

Of all the Old English words corresponding to Latin *secessus* and *latrina* perhaps only *heolstor* is euphemistic. Its primary sense, recorded several times in poetry and prose, is 'place of concealment', as, for example, when Grendel *wolde on heolster flēon* (*Beowulf*, 755), 'Grendel wished to find a hiding-place', in order to rejoin the *dēofla gedræg* (the company of demons). There is no suggestion whatever of a *double entendre* in any of them. The wide range of euphemistic synonyms to do with easement, privacy, comfort, convenience, running water, separation of the sexes (in public lavatories), and so on, were to come at intervals, as they became released from speech into print, in the centuries after the Conquest. I shall return to them later.

Anglo-Saxon kennings like *mere-hrægl*, 'sail' (literally 'sea-garment'), *freoðu-webbe*, 'woman' (literally 'weaver of peace'—by dynastic marriages), and *hron-rād*, 'sea' (literally 'riding-place of the whale') were not true euphemisms but rather condensed simile-compounds. Litotes (understatement) is fairly common but is usually not marked by the employment of 'pleasant or auspicious' words for 'unpleasant or inauspicious' ones. In *The Dream of the Rood*, for example, the dead body of Our Lord 'remained with a scanty retinue' (*reste he ðær mæte weorode*), that is, by a delicate use of litotes, 'alone'. Only now and then a streak of euphemism is discernible, as in the use of *ellorsīð*, 'death' (literally 'journey elsewhere'):

> Symble bið gemyndgad   morna gehwylce
> eaforan ellorsīð
>
> > (*Beowulf*, 2450–1)
>
> He is ever reminded each morning
> Of his son's death.

Some other synonyms for *die* (for example, *swefan*, mentioned above) and *death* (for example, *ealdor-gedāl* and *līf-gedāl*, both literally meaning 'separation from life') tend towards the euphemistic. The verb *(ge)cringan* 'to fall in battle, to die' may also have been contextually euphemistic. It originally meant 'to curl up' and is related by a slightly devious route to the verb *cringe*. Scholars will doubtless discover other examples of euphemisms in Old English.

The medical writers of the period used a wide range of mostly explicit terminology for the excretory and sexual organs and functions. Synonyms of *ears* (arse) include *ears-endu* (pl., buttocks) and (doubtless euphemistic) *setl* (seat). The anus is *ears-þerl* (*þerl* =*þyrel*, 'hole'). The entrails were *bæc-þearm* ('back intestines', cf. German *Darm*), *smeoru-þearm* (*smeoru*, 'fat, grease', etc.), and *snǣdel-þearm* (*snǣd*, piece cut off, slice). The degrees of intimacy or delicacy implied in such terminology and also in the synonyms for the genitalia are difficult to determine. The etymological meaning of the words is only partially helpful. Thus *gesceapu* in

> His gesceapu maðan weollon
>
> His private parts swarmed with vermin

etymologically means 'a shape, something made or shaped'. Other synonyms for the male genitalia included *getāwa* ('instruments') and *geweald* (where the underlying sense is 'power, control'). The occurrence of the phrase *geswell þāra gewalda*, 'the swelling of the *geweald*', is a clinical reminder that erection occurred then as now. The normal word for the female genitalia was *gecyndelic*:

> Gyf wīf cennan ne mæge, nime þysse wyrte wōs mid wulle, dō on þā gecyndelican.
>
> If a woman cannot conceive, take this herbal extract with wool and apply it to the pudenda.

Testicles were *herðan* (etymologically related to *heorða*, 'deer- (or goat-?) skin'), and the penis is variously *lim* (limb), *teors* (tarse), and *wǣpen* (weapon). Among the synonyms for sexual intercourse are *hǣmed* (the underlying idea being 'cohabitation'; cf. *hām*, 'home'), *hǣmedlāc* (*lāc*, 'play'), *hǣmedðing*, *wīf-gemāna* (*gemāna*, 'companionship, conjunction'), and *wīflāc* (*lāc*, 'play'). In the well-known passage in the *Anglo-Saxon Chronicle* about Cynewulf and Cyneheard, the phrase *þā geāscode hē þone cyning lytle werode on wīfcyþþe on Merantūne* may mean 'then he discovered the king having intercourse with a woman [rather than 'in the company of a woman'] at Merton', but the meaning is disputed.

Arguments based on etymological considerations are in the end indecisive. We may not even conclude that any colloquial connotations were attached to the word *mōnaðlican*, 'menstruation', despite its formal correspondence to modern 'monthlies', nor is it wise to assume any of the informality of the modern expression 'the curse' in the Anglo-Saxon word *mōnaðādl* (literally 'monthly illness').

The absence of any Anglo-Saxon literary works about infidelity or harlotry means that the terminology of Anglo-Saxon debauchery and licentiousness lies buried in obscurity. Not more than about ten synonyms for 'harlot' survive, probably none of them euphemistic. It is of interest to set them down in tabular form beside ten of the more usual terms of the present day.

OLD ENGLISH	MODERN ENGLISH
bepæcestre (seducer; cf. *pæcan*, to deceive)	*broad*
cifes (concubine; cf. mod. German *Kebser*)	*harlot*†
*cwene**	*hooker*
firenhicgend (harlot, adulteress)	*prostitute*
forlig(n)is (cf. *forlicgan*, to fornicate)	*scrubber*
*hōre**	*slag*
portcwene (town whore)	*slut*
scand (also 'shame, scandal')	*strumpet*†
scrætte (from Latin *scratta*)	*tart*
synnecge (used of Mary Magdalene)	*whore*
* Surviving as *quean* and *whore*	† Both now somewhat archaic

Only one word now appears in both lists, namely *hōre/whore*. In both groups the apportionment of sin is explicit: there is no holding back and no concealment. The difference is that in Old English these were the *only* recorded words for a prostitute. Old English *cifes* survived in the form *cheve(s)* into Middle English but is not recorded after 1400. With the exception of *cwene* and *hōre* none of the other words is recorded after the Conquest. Social attitudes changed. Prostitution became cloaked in new synonymy.

At all periods hard unforgiving words for prostitute have existed. But, as the centuries passed, evasive alternative words have emerged in profusion, expressions like *call girl*, *fallen woman*, *fille de joie, hostess, lady of easy virtue, model, moll, pick-up, street-walker,* and *woman of the town,* brought into being by social exigencies of the time. The mechanisms that released them were the same as those which governed the currency of 'fair-spoken' words for the private parts of the body and their functions. As the urban population increased, and social arrangements became more complex, the heavy sin-based terminology of the Anglo-Saxons went into desuetude. The new seams to be explored and exploited were those of gentility and politeness. New forms of etiquette replaced the old.

6. *Releasing mechanisms*

The monks, *scops* (poets), and ordinary citizens of the Anglo-Saxon period went to the *gang* (privy) (or the *gang-pytt,* etc.). Their descendants after the Conquest were able to draw upon a wider range of synonyms, though the native word *gang* remained in use throughout the medieval period:

. . . bordels of thise fool wommen . . . mowe be likned to a commune *gong,* where as men purgen hire ordure.

(Chaucer, *The Parson's Tale,* 885)

Gallicism in itself was a releasing mechanism: the new language (French) brought new words. In Chaucer's legend of Ariadne, for example, Theseus is thrown into a tower:

The tour, ther as this Theseus is throwe
Doun in the botom derk and wonder lowe,
Was joynynge in the wal to a *foreyne.*

(*The Legend of Good Women,* ll. 1960–2)

The *foreyne* (or *foreign*) is short for *chambre foreyne,* an outer privy. Chaucer, the releaser of so much informal vocabulary that before him was presumably restricted to the spoken language, boldly introduces euphemisms into his works. In *The Merchant's Tale* the young bride May declares that she must go 'Ther as ye woot that every wight moot neede' ('where, as you know, everyone must needs go'):

And whan she of this bille [sc. a letter from her lover] hath taken heede,
She rente it al to cloutes atte laste,
And in the *pryvee* softly it caste.

In *The Prioress's Tale* a widow's seven-year-old son is murdered and his body disposed of:

> I seye that in a *wardrobe* [sc. privy] they hym threwe
> Where-as thise Jewes purgen hire entraille.

The word *privy* has survived. Chaucer's other synonyms did not.

Shakespeare's latrine vocabulary is relatively restrained. Costard's use of *Ajax* to mean 'a jakes' is well known:

> your lion, that holds his poll-axe sitting on a close-stool, will be given to Ajax . . .   (*Love's Labour's Lost*, v. ii. 581)

And the word *jakes* itself is used in an undisguised manner in *King Lear* (II. ii. 70) when Kent says that he will 'tread this unbolted villain [sc. Oswald] into mortar, and daub the wall of a jakes with him'. Less well known are Scarus's use of *bench-hole*: 'We'll beat 'em into *bench-holes* . . .' (*Antony and Cleopatra*, IV. vii. 9) and Timon's

> Hang them or stab them, drown them in a *draught* (*Timon of Athens*, v. i. 105)

A *draught* or *draught-house* was an acceptably neutral or even a slightly genteel term to judge from the fact that the compilers of the Authorized Version (1611) preferred *draught-house* (2 Kings 10: 27) to Coverdale's *prevy house*.

After Shakespeare's time releasing mechanisms of one kind or another multiplied the terminology to a quite extraordinary extent. The multiplication of terms and the century in which they were first recorded are shown in the following tables:

1600–1699	*1700–1799*	*1800–1899*
closet	bog(s)	bog-house
commons	dunniken, dunny	convenience
gingerbread-office	head(s) (on a ship)	earth closet
latrine	little house	toilet
necessary house, place, etc.	necessary (as a noun)	WC
	office	
	water-closet	

1900–	
bathroom*	comfort station*
can*	Gentlemen
cloaks	gents

1900–

geography of the house	lavatory
	lavvy
john, johnny*	loo
karzy	men's room*
Ladies	public convenience
lav	rest room*
lavabo	

* Chiefly US

These lists are not exhaustive but they show the outline of the semantic area filled by synonyms for privy, including those that are euphemistic, from Old English *gang* to modern socially divisive expressions like *comfort station* and *rest room* (US genteel), *loo* and *the geography of the house* (UK middle and upper middle class), and *toilet* (UK working class and lower middle class).

The historical trail of the harlot runs from Old English *cifes* and *hōre* to modern English *prostitute* and *whore*. Wave after wave of social prudery at times drove the more explicit terms into retreat, while other social mechanisms brought them back in use and also generated new hard-core words.

In the sixteenth-century the following more or less specific synonyms for prostitute came into the language:

baggage	hackney	public woman
cat	*hiren	pucelle
cockatrice	*hobby-horse	punk
cony	laced mutton	*stale (noun)
courtesan	limmer	*stew
doxy	loon	street-walker
drab	minx	tomboy
*driggle-draggle	mort	wagtail
*flirt-gill	mutton	

(Those marked * were short-lived: none of these is recorded after 1660. Others remained in the language for only a slightly longer period.)

Other synonyms or near-synonyms for prostitute were first recorded in the following periods:

1600–1699		1700–1799
buttock	crack	demi-rep
cousin	customer	fille de joie

1600–1699		1700–1799	
fireship	prostitute	lady of easy	
flap	pug	virtue	
lady of pleasure	strum	rake	
marmalade-	tomrig	woman of the	
madam	town-woman	town	
night-walker	vizard		
nymph (of the	waistcoateer		
pavement)			

1800–1899		1900–	
buer	hooker	brass nail	make (noun)
chippy	horizontal (noun)	broad	model
cocotte	horse-breaker	call girl	muff
demi-mondaine	pick-up	demi-vierge	pavement
fallen woman	scarlet woman	demi-virgin	princess
flagger	tart	hostess	scrub
flapper	unfortunate	hump	scrubber
	(noun)	lay (noun)	slag

The language of the sexual organs and of sexual play has darted into and out of the language as puritanism retreated and advanced. The first major unprudish woman in English literature is Chaucer's Wife of Bath. As she observes, the 'membres of generacion' were 'nat maad for noght':

> Glose whoso wole, and seye bothe up and doun,
> That they were maked for purgacioun
> Of uryne, and oure bothe thynges smale
> Were eek to knowe a femele from a male,
> And for noon oother cause,—say ye no?
>
> *(The Wife of Bath's Prologue, 119–23)*

She revels in the language of 'bothe thynges smale':

> For, certeyn, olde dotard, by youre leve,
> Ye shul have *queynte* right ynogh at eve.
>
> (Ibid., 331–2)

Her *queynte* is also, euphemistically, her *bele chose* (447), *quoniam* (608), and *chambre of Venus* (618). It is hardly a circuitous journey from this kind of language and from the euphemistic indirectness of *The Miller's Tale*:

> And thus lith Alison and Nicholas,
> In bisynesse of myrthe and of solas . . .
>
> (3653–4)

and of

> And shortly for to seyn, they were aton
>
> *(The Reeve's Tale*, 4197)

to the euphemizing of Dryden, Sterne, and Fielding mentioned above and to that of other writers in later centuries. What changed from generation to generation was the prominence given either to explicit language or to language that was more reserved. Both kinds co-existed but advanced or retreated according to the mode of the writer or the mood of the age.

7. *The printed word unchained*

The limitless expansion of the printed word in the present century possibly makes it seem as if the proportion of euphemisms (and of every other kind of rhetorical device) has increased considerably. But this is not necessarily so. Previous centuries are now closed periods. For the most part the vocabulary that can be collected in a methodical way from them has been collected. They are not always obliging centuries, and many of the verbal patterns of the past are buried beyond the reach of analysis. In the nine hundred years or so since the Norman Conquest it is easy enough to discern the main forces (or releasing mechanisms as I have called them) which have caused successive generations to bring new 'well-omened' expressions into being and to abandon or suppress other more explicit ones. Avoidance of unseemly words springs from a deeply instinctive belief that by so doing one will gradually cause them to disappear, or at any rate make the concepts denoted by them seem to be less intrusive. War, death, politics, birth, fornication, bodily functions like excretion, reticence, social rank and other social relationships—these and other primary matters have generated 'well-sounding' and 'harsh-sounding' expressions down through the centuries.

Our present age, like those of the past, produces euphemisms to conceal or take attention away from its particular embarrassments and its unsolved problems. In the 1914–18 war *Big Bertha* was the name given, somewhat affectionately, to a field-gun of immense destructive power. In North Africa during the 1939–45 war troops seemed to be forever 'retiring to prepared positions'. Public fears needed to be allayed, at least until the story changed at El Alamein. Our fighter pilots 'bought it' or 'went for a Burton' as they crashed and were killed. The highly vulnerable gunners at the rear end of bomber planes came to be affectionately known as 'tail-end Charlies'. In the Vietnam war the Americans discovered the calming usefulness of expressions like *pacification* (destruction of villages and evacuation of the inhabitants) and *defoliation* (destruction of forests used by the enemy as cover). In the Falklands campaign a cluster bomb used by the RAF consisted of more than a hundred bomblets, each of which when exploded disintegrated into hundreds of high-velocity fragments dispersed over a wide area.

The effect on what are euphemistically called *soft-skinned targets*—a category which includes people—is devastating. (*London Review of Books*, 15 Sept.–5 Oct. 1983)

None of these processes of soft-naming is new or particularly alarming. Almost any act or deed can be described factually or without connotations of any kind. Equally almost everything can be subtly altered for better or worse if a speaker or writer wishes this to happen. At any given time a battery of substitutional words or phrases exists, to be made use of, kept in reserve, or avoided, at choice. A language without euphemisms would be a defective instrument of communication.

Sir John Betjeman's poem 'Churchyards' reminds us that death is still a primary source of euphemisms:

> Oh why do people waste their breath
> Inventing dainty names for death?
> On the old tombstones of the past
> We do not read 'At peace at last'
> But simply 'died' or plain 'departed'.

Much of the ancient sense of sin has been removed from suicide. Yet Arthur Koestler's death-note written in June 1982 used the euphemism 'seek self-deliverance' as a synonym for 'commit suicide' and 'put an end to my life', both of which phrases also occurred. *Self-deliverance*, taken by Koestler from the vocabulary of the group known as Exit, deserves to be ranked with the funereal vocabulary brought into prominence by Evelyn Waugh in *The Loved One* (1948): the Happier Hunting Ground (for a dead Sealyham terrier), the Slumber Room of the Whispering Glades Memorial Park, the Radiant Childhood Smile restored to the face of Sir Francis Hinsley (who had hanged himself and by doing so grossly distorted his features).

Sexual matters are less hedged about with 'fair-spoken' words than they once were. But race bristles with them, and even the phrase *race relations* itself is seen by Nadine Gordimer as a euphemism. Among the sad figures in her *Burger's Daughter* (1979) is an 'old-maid schoolteacher' anxious to do uplifting work in the black townships of South Africa:

Something less self-defeating than charity, for what (euphemism being their natural means of expression) they call 'race relations'.

There is no shortage of euphemisms in the more casual areas of life. 'Do you drink?' is apparently an underworld expression for asking a policeman if he will take a bribe. Emily, in R. Jaffe's *Class Reunion* (1979), 'hated being "petite", which was a euphemism for getting stuck with all the short boys on blind dates'. A recent issue of the journal *Maledicta* reported that 'a tall building' is sometimes used as a euphemism for an erection. An American bank is said to have avoided the dreaded word 'loss' by calling it a 'net profits revenue deficiency'. In some quarters drug addicts have come to be called 'dependents with a chemical problem'. These minor evasions are of a piece with the avoidance of the word 'leg' a century or more ago:

I am not so particular as some people are, for I know those who always say limb of a table, or limb of a piano-forte.

(Frederick Marryat, *Diary in America*, 1839)

This over-delicate preference has been abandoned. But it has left a tiny legacy in that a common term for an artificial leg (or arm) is still an artificial *limb*, whether or not it replaces one that had been a 'soft-skinned target' or one that had been removed for some other reason.

REFERENCES

The Oxford English Dictionary, 1884–1933, and supplementary volumes, 1972–86
Eric Partridge, *Shakespeare's Bawdy*, 1947 and later editions
Rochester's Poems on Several Occasions, ed. James Thorpe, 1950
G. L. Brook, *The Language of Dickens*, 1970
The Forbidden Erotica of Thomas Rowlandson, introduced by Kurt von Meier, 1970
Ralph W. V. Elliott, *Chaucer's English*, 1974
G. L. Brook, *The Language of Shakespeare*, 1976

Norman Davies *et al.*, *A Chaucer Glossary*, 1979
Hugh Rawson, *A Dictionary of Euphemisms and Other Doubletalk*, 1981
Judith S. Neaman and Carole G. Silver, *A Dictionary of Euphemisms*, 1983
   (in US, *Kind Words: A Thesaurus of Euphemisms*)

3

Topics

Meaningful abbreviations

When I was in Peking in 1979 I met many lexicographers and linguistic scholars who insisted that, among other things, makers of dictionaries should go out into the streets and factories to find out from the people themselves—street-sweepers and foundry workers, for example—what particular words actually meant as distinct from what lexicographers thought they meant. I told them that I had done just that on occasion, for example by visiting an oil well in Wiltshire and by pestering everyone I met socially about the true meaning of the word or words I happened to be working on at the time. The net result was that a small number of words went into the Oxford dictionaries in marginally better shape than they would otherwise have done.

There are, however, various classes of words and names that change their meaning or their nature so rapidly or unobtrusively that more than ordinary vigilance is required. Thus, for example, Upper Volta became an independent republic in 1960 but changed its name to Burkina-Faso in 1984. Its capital, mercifully, is still called Ouagadougou. Suriname, Dhaka (capital of Bangladesh), and Vanuatu are now the official names of what were once called Surinam, Dacca, and the New Hebrides. The Marriage Guidance Council has changed its name to Relate. Doubtless, official notice of the changes was given in all appropriate places, but it takes a while for good reliable dictionaries to keep up with events.

One class of abbreviations that is less subject to change, but which dictionaries usually ignore is the code used in foreign countries to clarify spelling on the telephone. For example, I was amused to hear a hotel receptionist in Florence spell out my name on the telephone as *B* for Bologna, *U* for Urbino, *R* for Roma, and so on down to *D* for Domodossola.

Dictionaries are almost totally unhelpful when it comes to unravelling the abbreviations used in the personal advertisements.

I first noticed the ubiquitous abbreviations used in the personal column of the *New York Review of Books*. For example: 'New York Lawyer, SJM, 39, seeks warm, friendly SJF 21–41, interested in travel, theater, music, opera, etc.'; 'Central Jersey DWJF, 41, Ph.D., Professional, parent of 2 teen-aged girls. Attractive, warm, looking for compatible man to share social, cultural, family life.' No current British or American standard dictionary lists 'SJM', 'SJF', 'DWJF', or any of the other similar sets of abbreviations used in these colourful and imaginative advertisements.

I turned to the *London Review of Books*. It lists Readers' Requests, Lectures, Houses for Sale or Rent, and Services ('Unfindable books found', 'Spanish lessons offered by native speaker', 'Literate word processing and DTP (= desk top publishing) services', but obviously does not permit the seeking of 'warm, friendly relationships' through classified ads. *The Times* admits advertisements from agencies: 'A very special lady seeks a very special man . . . We have established ourselves as the most prestigious introduction service in Britain . . . We are not a dating agency . . .' No dating, definitely not. It does have a column devoted to Flatshare advertisements, though, and in these, cheek by jowl with obvious abbreviations (Dble rm, grd flr flat, Nr stn) are some that are somewhat opaque: C/H (= central heating), n/s (= non-smoker), O/R (= own room), W/M (= washing machine). M/F, of course, means 'male or female', and Prof means 'professional' not 'Professor'—it seems unlikely that half a dozen professors a day are seeking accommodation in central London and thereabouts.

The *New Statesman* is perhaps the most hospitable of the upper-echelon publications in its listings of a personal kind (under the heading 'Heartsearch'). Thus, for example, 'Plumpish, Liberalist, impoverished male, 31, cat-fan, still Guardian-reading after all these years, seeks similar female, London/SE. Help, I may be turning into a Kingsley Amis character!'; 'Gay graduate, nearly-anglicized Italian, 40 (looks younger), enjoys art and travel, seeks guy, 28–40, for meaningful relationship. Photo appreciated.' But there are no obfuscating abbreviations.

I asked the editor of the *New York Review of Books*, Barbara Epstein, for a key to all their personal column abbreviations. Here they are (in alphabetical order): Bi (Bisexual); D (Divorced), F (Female), G (Gay), J (Jewish), JNR (Jewish, not religious), M (Male), M (Married), S (Single), S/D (Single or Divorced), W (White). Because M has two meanings it is customary to separate them

when they are needed in the same advertisement: MJM (= Married
Jewish Male), MWM (= Married White Male). The list seems to
cover most circumstances. I hope that it may prevent someone in
the future from making the wrong assumptions. Dictionaries in all
English-speaking countries may like to make a note of them. There
is considerable room for improvement in their treatment of this
area of vocabulary.

Sunday Times 9 April 1989

Adverbs ending in -*edly*

'We accept that this was not the case and unreservedly apologize to
——': thus the normal formula when a newspaper offers apologies
to a person whose views have been misrepresented. Count the
syllables in 'unreservedly' and everyone, I imagine, would say five.
'Dickensian insolvency laws match their unembarrassedly Victorian
values' (David Jessel in a recent issue of the *Listener*). Unembarrassedly? Five syllables or six? The answer is not easy. '"Oh yes,"
says the boy, shamefacedly, "that's all right."' (*OED*, 1881.) The
going begins to look hard.

David Jessel's sentence caught my eye because I am trying to
decide how comprehensively I must rewrite Fowler's essay on
-*edly* (and also his cross-references) in my forthcoming new edition
of *Modern English Usage*.

Consider the size of the problem. In *MEU*, Fowler gave nearly
three columns to -*edly* and inserted some seventy cross-references
to the article itself. His choice of examples seems highly idiosyncratic, especially when measured against the *OED*, but that by
the by.

Of Fowler's seventy, the ones that have stood in the language
longest are *advisedly*, *assuredly*, and *unadvisedly*, all first recorded
in the fourteenth century. Further waves of such words came along
in the sixteenth century (*amazedly*, *ashamedly*, *deservedly*,
learnedly, etc.), the seventeenth century (*avowedly*, *designedly*,
reservedly, *resignedly*, etc.), and the eighteenth century (*animatedly*,
detachedly, *vexedly*, etc.). But the great age of -*edly* was the
nineteenth century: no fewer than twenty-one of Fowler's seventy
are first recorded then (*absorbedly*, *allegedly*, *presumedly*, *un-
abashedly*, etc.), and under *markedly* the *OED* adds the comment
'a favourite 19th c. adverb'. Two are not recorded in the *OED*

before the present century (*painedly*, 1921, *unashamedly*, 1905), as is also the case with *reportedly* (1901), not mentioned by Fowler.

Some of those listed by Fowler now seem very abstruse, e.g. *admiredly*, *discomposedly*, *harassedly*, and *labouredly*. He also lists ten words that are not recorded in the *OED* at all (e.g. *advancedly*, *annoyedly*, *ascertainedly*, *incensedly*, *mystifiedly*).

Certain patterns emerge when tests are applied to Fowler's seventy words. A fully pronounced *-ed-* is obligatory in the great majority, no matter how many syllables there are in the word. Thus, *learnedly* and *markedly* would always have three syllables, and *advisedly*, *assuredly*, *deservedly*, *reservedly*, and *resignedly* would always have four, while the majority of words beginning with the prefix *un-* would normally have five (e.g. *unashamedly*, *unconcernedly*, *unreservedly*), though this obviously depends on the nature of the main part of the word.

Such words are frequently formed on the past tense or past participle of the corresponding verb. Thus *allege* → *alleged* → *allegedly*. In some cases such adverbs are extensions of adjectives, e.g. *belatedly*, *conceitedly*, *shamefacedly*. In still others the formations are parasynthetic (i.e. contain two different parts of speech), e.g. *cold-bloodedly*, *high-handedly*, *whole-heartedly*, all three, incidentally, nineteenth-century formations, and all regularly pronounced as four syllables. The similar formations *good-naturedly* and *good-humouredly* entered the language a century earlier, but these are normally pronounced with just four syllables, not five.

There is a residue of *-edly* words in which the problem of pronouncing or not pronouncing the *-ed-* remains. Here is the test, or the beginnings of it. How would D. H. Lawrence have pronounced 'painedly' in his *England, My England* (1921)? How would Browning and Kipling respectively have pronounced 'starchedly' (*Red Cotton Night-Cap Country*, 1873) and 'subduedly' (*The Light that Failed*, 1891)? And how many syllables are to be pronounced in the following words, all listed from standard sources in the *OED*: *admiredly*, *depressedly*, *dissatisfiedly*, *harassedly*, *labouredly*, *preoccupiedly*, *scatteredly*, *studiedly*, *unembarrassedly*, and *veiledly*? Does anyone know for certain? Or is it all just a matter of personal preference and contextual convenience? Perhaps we need a full-scale opinion poll to find out whether people pronounce 'unembarrassedly' as five syllables or six and 'shame-facedly' as three syllables or four?

Sunday Times 4 February 1990

Compound adverbs

Late in their life some of our adverbs are being reshuffled. Standoffish pairs of adverbs, once always kept apart, are being brought together and it is not only the Americans who are responsible.

Let me begin, out of alphabetical order, with the most serious of the arranged marriages. After the adoption of the Dutch word *onderweg* in the mid-eighteenth century, our ships, away from their moorings, were said to be 'under way'. About forty years later, some people connected with the sea, cleverly but erroneously, associated the phrase with the weighing of anchors and used 'under weigh' instead. They were followed by myriads of writers, including Thackeray ('But though the steamer was under weigh, he might not be on board', *Vanity Fair*, ch. LXVII). For nearly two centuries, writers, whether of the 'way' or the 'weigh' camp, regularly wrote the expression as two words, 'under way' or 'under weigh': thus Captain Marryat, Washington Irving, Byron, Carlyle, and many others. Then something happened. The mysterious force that in earlier centuries had brought a great many other adverbs together (*any* + *way* → *anyway*) struck again. Ships, projects, experiments—almost anything—from the 1930s onward began in some circles to get 'underway'. Uncle Sam was partly to blame but so was John Bull in the form of some of our most competent young writers—Martin Amis and William Boyd, for instance. From the latter: 'They walked arm-in-arm into the club where the dance was underway.' And from a 1987 issue of the *New York Review of Books*: 'America's declared foreign policy of fostering stability . . . in Central America might at last get underway.' The joined-up form is now in American dictionaries. The style books of the Oxford University Press and of *The Economist* still firmly, and quite rightly, recommend 'two words'. So will you hold back, please, you young British novelists? We are not quite ready for this arranged marriage yet. In the twenty-first century perhaps.

The next one is a bit of a muddle, let's face it. *Straight* (which is in origin an adjectival use of the medieval past participle of *stretch* and has nothing to do with its homonym *strait*) is first recorded in conjunction with *away*—as two separate words—in 1662: some prisoners 'were hurri'd streight away to their Quarters'. As an adverbial form it stayed that way, as two separate words, until the beginning of the present century. Then, while nobody was looking, a marriage of the two words was arranged. In 1923, for example, the *Daily Mail* reported that a horse called Evander had been badly hurt and was 'straightaway' withdrawn from a race. A character in Marghanita Laski's *Tory Heaven* (1948) followed with 'I said straightaway . . . that I'd like to be a land-agent'. 'I'll buy some straightaway,' said Gina solemnly in Thomas Keneally's novel *A Family Madness* (1985). Bernice Rubens's crazy hero Mr Wakefield (1985) 'rang the bell straightaway, to give himself no opportunity for second thoughts'. For my part, I still like to see fresh air between the two words, but a certificate of marriage may have to be issued soon. The trouble is that the Americans, or those of them who know about horse-racing, use *straightaway* as a noun meaning 'a straight section of a racecourse'. And the noun is not restricted to racecourses.

Regular readers of the *New Yorker* (a linguistically conservative magazine) will know that the customary form of 'any more' in its pages is *anymore*: 'He doesn't go to funerals anymore'; 'we don't call them wigs or hairpieces anymore', both from recent issues. The joined-up form is entered in American dictionaries with reservations about its distribution and level. *Collins English Dictionary* (1986) signposts the use as 'esp. US'. It may well appear one day in the *Concise Oxford Dictionary* but is not there yet. The use has spread to less well-mapped areas like New Zealand, to judge from 'God, no jokes even in this hut anymore!' in Vincent O'Sullivan's terrifying play *Shuriken* (1985). Nevertheless it is still the kind of conjoined form that brings British readers up with a start, in the manner of *alright* (for 'all right'). Penelope Lively, in her Booker Prize novel *Moon Tiger* displays a proper conservatism in the matter: 'He is not lying there any more'.

In all three cases separate elements are being brought together by a process that has been happening for centuries. The language is littered with compound adverbs, most of which were once normally written as two words: *anyway, furthermore, overboard, whatsoever,* and so on. More arranged marriages will doubtless occur in the centuries ahead. Perhaps some trendy novelist will start the ball rolling with (for example) *byandlarge, earlyon, onandoff, thereandthen,* or *toandfro*. They look crazy, but then so, to many people in this country, do *anymore, straightaway,* and (especially) *underway*.

Sunday Times 21 February 1988

Recruitment advertising

At the beginning of 1988 I examined the linguistic conventions used in some supplements to the *Sunday Times* containing advertisements for appointments at a senior level. The style used was doubtless familiar to people in the recruitment advertising trade, and presumably also to suitable applicants for the jobs, but much of it was new to me.

Easily the most popular term for a senior post turned out to be 'Manager', but it seemed never to be used by itself. It was always preceded by qualifying words: Systems Development Manager, Group Information Services Manager, Product Development Manager, Distributor Support Manager, Technical Operations Manager.

It was not at all clear whether a 'Director' these days is more senior or less senior than a 'Manager', but it too was normally preceded by a qualifying word: Advertisement Director, Finance Director, Sales Director, Technical Director.

'Managing Directors' were relatively rare and it was noticeable that the inevitable qualifying words were placed *after* the main title: Managing Director Manufacturing, Managing Director Conferences, Managing Director, Marketing Subsidiary.

One or two posts contained the word 'Executive'. These, as it happened, had the qualifying words in front: Chief Executive, Marketing Executive, Sales Executive, Senior Executive, High Technology Venture Capital Executive. It seems that a job title can easily attract as many as five run-together words.

Coming down a cog or two, there were vacancies for analysts, consultants, controllers, project leaders, specialists, team leaders, and so on, but it was clear that these were not the *crème de la crème*.

The salaries offered were presented in a variety of styles: c£30,000, to £37,000, up to £16.7K, c£30K OTE, £35,000 GTE, £27,000 Basic. To job-seekers at this level the abbreviations OTE and GTE are presumably familiar: apparently they stand for 'on target earnings' and 'guaranteed target earnings'.

Most of the advertisements gave an indication of the 'package' going with the salary: this was called 'benefits' (or 'major benefits' or 'excellent benefits'), a 'rewards package', a 'compensation package', or a 'competitive package'.

The most frequent lure by far was a company car, described with varying degrees of boastfulness: '+ car', '+ quality car', '+ executive car', '+ expensed 2.0L car', '+ prestige car'. Other bribes included 'relocation help' (or 'relocation costs/expenses'), BUPA[1] premiums, and profit share.

Applicants were required to have certain skills or qualifications, and the request was usually expressed in future time, with the applicant directly addressed in the second person: 'you will be able to demonstrate good presentation', 'you will have a strong record of achievement', 'you will have exceptional interpersonal communication skills'. Sometimes the word 'must' was used: 'you must have a good technical degree', 'you must be articulate, confident, and resilient', but this use, one feels, was adopted with qualms and only in extreme circumstances. Better to fall back, one can hear the advertiser saying, on 'will' rather than on 'must' or 'should'. Only an old buffer, grappling with competing styles, could have come up with the wordy formula 'it is most likely that candidates will have worked in the computer industry'. The most conservative advertisements used 'should' and the third person: 'applicants should be in their 30s'. The successful applicant for this post is likely to find himself or herself dealing with an old fogey of a personnel manager.

Naturally technical and scientific businesses expected their applicants to know the jargon of the occupation: so computer terms like 'IT' (= information technology), 'MIS' (= management information system), and 'UNIX' (= a trademark for an operation system for certain minicomputers) were left unexplained.

One of the most frequent adjectives used in the advertisements was 'proven': applicants will have 'proven expertise' or 'proven ability'.

There is a gradient of politeness in the manner in which the personnel officer described himself or herself. A few gallantly kept to the older conventions (Miss Martin, Mr R. J. Walsh). The great majority adopted a much more informal style, with no prefixes at all: Maggie Munday, Terry Toms, Sharon Jolly, Chris Mossop, Nicola Ogilvie, and so on. There was not a single example of Ms and only one of Mrs.

As far as I could see, most of the public sector advertisers declared themselves to be 'an equal opportunities employer': thus British Telecom, the Electricity Council, the NHS Training

---

[1] BUPA, the British United Provident Association, a private medical insurance scheme.

Authority, and so on. Only Allied Dunbar, of all the advertisers, spelt out what this formula means: 'Applications are welcome regardless of sex, marital status, ethnic origin or disability.' The others were silent on the subject.

The vocabulary of senior positions and of advertisements for such posts naturally reflects the market economy of the society in which we live. Its mysteries are not always explained by even our largest dictionaries. Most readers must just gaze at abbreviations like £25KOQE£50K (in a management consultancy advertisement) and f.m.c.g. (in the supermarket trade) with a certain wonderment, and wait for the dictionaries to catch up. But to save the lexicographers time and trouble, I have established that OQE stands for 'on quota earnings' and f.m.c.g. for 'fast moving consumer goods'.

In our high-tech society such is the way that top-level appointments, duties, and privileges are now described. It is a quickly invented golden comfortable world, beckoningly attractive to those who are seeking to move into it. I tried out 'OTE' and 'OQE' on two successful young businessmen in Oxford and drew a blank. So some of the language is aimed at chrysalis yuppies rather than fully-fledged ones. It also occurred to me to wonder what those with long titles entered on their passports and other official documents. 'High Technology Venture Capital Executive'? Hardly. Perhaps 'Tech Exec'? Or, dash it all, just 'Executive'?

Sunday Times 7 February 1988

Archaisms

Archaism seems to be a necessary component of the language. At any given time modes of expression and of word formation are retained long after it would seem likely that their sell-by date had passed. At all levels of writing, one finds words, phrases, old verbal endings, strange orderings of words lifted out of old books as reminders of earlier centuries. Some are obvious echoes of Shakespeare. Others—especially the use of the verbal terminations *-est* and *-eth*—remind us of the Authorized Version of the Bible. Some seem to have stepped into standard English from the private haunts of regional dialects.

Archaic spellings lie dotted about the language. Thus (in

imitation of Isaak Walton's title) *The Compleat Bachelor* (the title
of a book by Oliver Onions, 1900); 'She writes and sings and paints
and dances and plays I don't know how many instruments. The
compleat girl' (Mary McCarthy, 1963); 'The Compleat Hiker's
Checklist' (*Modern Maturity*, an American magazine, 1988). Other
spellings suggest a sturdy antiquity: the Canterbury Clerkes,
Whitaker's Almanack, the Culham Fayre; and, of course, a
multitude of uses with 'olde', e.g. 'A lot of olde realle beames in
Amersham and a lot of olde phonie cookynge too' (*Good Food
Guide*, 1959); 'Charming stone built olde worlde cottage of
immense character' (*Rhyl Journal & Advertiser*, 1976).

Long-abandoned verbal inflexions are used to add a contextual
element of antiquity: 'If Mimi's cup runneth over, it runneth over
with decency rather than with anything more vital' (Anita
Brookner, 1985—cf. Psalm 23: 5); 'Horrid new world. That hath
such creatures in't' (Janice Elliott, 1985—cf. *The Tempest*, v. i.
183); 'The whole creation groaneth and travaileth in pain together'
(Iris Murdoch, 1987—cf. Romans 8: 22).

Normal word order is disturbed, often as a deliberately archaistic
device: 'Tibba still pined and slavered for the school lunches. And
little other care hath she' (A. N. Wilson, 1982); 'I would rinse out
somebody's mouth at Clairol loved I not honour more' (William
Safire, 1986).

Words that would normally be paint-stripped from the fresh
timber to which they cling abound, words like *anent, nay, twain,
yea*, and *yesteryear*: 'I joked to Dale anent publicity' (John Updike,
1986); 'So farewell then Durex shop at 34 Wardour Street, London
W.1, so named for your proud, nay brazen, storefront' (*The Face*,
1987): 'I intend to sleep for an hour or twain' (Paul Bailey, 1986);
'My heart bleeds for the thousands, yea, tens of thousands of men
and women in our penal and psychiatric institutions' (*Chicago
Tribune*, 1988); 'He spoke . . . of learned controversies and
misapprehensions of yesteryear' (Margaret Drabble, 1987).

The prefix *a-* with a present participle (a centuries-old type of
word formation) is having a new lease of life, a-basking in its
ubiquity: 'Kris Kirk . . . plans to return, a-brandishing the
manuscript, by the end of March' (*Melody Maker*, 1988); 'The
times they are a-changing' (Bob Dylan, 1960s); ' "Time's a-
wasting," said Ben. "What are we going to do?" ' (Anthony Lejeune,
1986); 'President Bush, who came a-wooing here [sc. in Germany]
just two weeks ago' (*Spectator*, 1989). The *OED*'s note restricting

this type of word to 'most of the southern dialects, and the vulgar speech both in England and America' is distinctly outmoded.

Perhaps everyone's favourite archaic-looking words, though, are *albeit* and *unbeknownst*. *Albeit* is a worn-down version of the conjunctive phrase 'all be it (that) (= let it entirely be that)'. Despite its antiquity it still has the look of a bone-crushed word, but it is frequently used: 'It is an unwelcome, albeit necessary, restraint' (Anthony Storr, 1972); '"Jesus!" they said in Italian albeit in a conversational manner' (Harry Secombe, 1981); 'A great line of poetry, albeit by a mendacious fascist, will outlast . . . the most sanctified of good deeds' (*Times Literary Supplement*, 1988).

Unknownst emerged from regional speech (especially in Ireland and the Isle of Man) in the early nineteenth century to stand as a vague threat to the standard word *unknown*. *Unbeknown* appeared earlier (first recorded in 1636) and remains as an occasional substitute for *unknown*. But the ungainly form *unbeknownst*, first recorded in a letter of Mrs Gaskell's written in 1848, has swept into prominence in all forms of English. The *OED* cites examples from Kipling, Synge, and William Faulkner, as well as from a 1982 issue of the *London Review of Books*. It now turns up everywhere like a prized piece of wreckage salvaged from a precious old vessel. Even in a novel called *Prisoners* (1987) by the Texan novelist Bill Ripley: 'In one of his experiments with the videos, Richard had drummed up a snuff-flick gang out of Colombia and, unbeknownst to Les, had a real live snuff tracked beneath a section of a Bill Cosby show.' This peasant-like word could not have been thrust into a more unrural context.

Sunday Times 7 January 1990

Big Bang[1]

After Big Bang (as the stockbrokers called it) it gradually emerged that the traditional distinction beten two central Stock Exchange terms, 'broker' and 'jobber' (and their unabbreviated forms 'stockbroker' and 'stockjobber'), had been officially abolished. It all sounded very neat and clinical.

I consulted the *OED* to see what complications this would cause

---

[1] Name given to some major changes made in late 1986 to the organization and practices of the City of London as Britain's financial centre.

and, sure enough, complications there were. There is no serious difficulty about 'brokeress', a term first used in 1583 as a female go-between or procuress, and from 1872 of a female stockbroker (in America, of course—it would be, wouldn't it?, I can hear British readers saying). For all I know both kinds will continue to call themselves brokeresses on their (American) passports, not heeding the message of Big Bang. There are no jobberesses in the Dictionary as far as I can see.

What about the various kinds of brokers who have up till now been distinguished from jobbers? 'Brokers of Exchange' are first recorded in 1622. The *OED* declares that 'brokers are divided into different classes, as "bill" or "exchange brokers", "stockbrokers", "ship" and "insurance brokers", "pawnbrokers"'. Other kinds of brokers, those dealing in commodities, like 'cotton-brokers', 'tea-brokers', and 'wood-brokers', also receive the full historical treatment in the Dictionary.

That was the first complication—this shipyardful of brokers, not all of them to be distinguished from jobbers.

The Stock Exchange itself has changed its name several times. As in other languages its first name was the 'Burse' (or Exchange) when it was built in London in 1566 by Sir Thomas Gresham, and it was officially called the Royal Exchange by Queen Elizabeth I. Just over two hundred years later it was renamed: 'Yesterday the Brokers and others at New Jonathan's, came to a resolution, that instead of its being called New Jonathan's, it should be named "The Stock Exchange", which is to be wrote over the door' (*London Chronicle* 13–15 July 1773).

I turned to Dr Johnson's Dictionary (1755) for illumination and found that he was more concerned with acerbity than with up-to-dateness. A stockjobber, according to Johnson, is 'a low wretch who gets money by buying and selling shares in the funds'. There is no entry for 'stockbroker' and none (not even in the editions issued later in his lifetime) for 'Royal Exchange' or 'Stock Exchange'.

Nowadays lexicographers are not permitted to be so lofty or so negligent. Big Bang has abolished a distinction, and the removal of this distinction has consequences for every dictionary in the land. 'Burnham' is another word that is likely soon to disappear from non-historical dictionaries if Kenneth Baker and the schoolteachers discard the old scale of salaries in favour of another.

Nothing of this is new. Lexicographers have already dealt with wave after wave of lexical changes since the war. 'Atomic' was once the customary adjective applied to the Bomb and to power stations. Now 'nuclear' is generally used, but, after Chernobyl, for how long? The Chicago writer Studs Terkel recently pointed out that 'slum' gave way in America to 'ghetto', and then, everywhere, to 'inner city'. Good dictionaries have removed, or are in the process of removing, 'Mohammedan', 'Asiatic', 'Negro', 'O-level', 'X' (and other classifications of film) from their definitions in favour of 'Muslim', 'Asian', 'Black', 'GCSE', and 'PG/15/18'. Metrication and decimalization, still at half-cock in Britain, have produced a labyrinth of lexical distinctions and tables of equivalents. Lexicographers need to be as vigilant as lighthouse-keepers or air traffic controllers. More Big Bangs lie ahead.

Daily Telegraph 24 November 1986

Cubs and whelps

One of my earliest school memories is of the pleasure we got from answering questions like 'What is the name of a baby cat, cow, duck, goose, hare, swan, wolf, etc.?' We all dutifully set down kitten, calf, duckling, gosling, leveret, cygnet, cub, etc., and thought the problem solved. The correspondences appeared to be neatly reciprocal. The name of each young creature seemed to be either quite distinct from that of the parent (horse: foal) or one that added or contained a diminutive suffix (pig: piglet). At that stage I am sure it never occurred to us that more complex linguistic factors might be at work.

First, some ground-clearing work. In lay language, many small creatures lack precise names distinct from those of their parents. At one time or another most of us tend to fall back on circumlocutions like baby elephant, baby giraffe, and baby snake. By contrast it is impressive to hear knowledgeable fishermen weaving words like botcher, grilse, parr, samlet, skegger, and skirling into their conversation when they are talking about the grade or age of young salmon. Ornithologists use various types of classification for the young of birds, to the bafflement of ordinary people. For example, some birds are altricial (= needing to be reared by the parents in the nest) or nidicolous (the same), while others are praecocial (= able to leave the nest and to feed themselves as soon as they are hatched). Pigeons and herons are altricial, while newly hatched plovers are praecocial.

The passage of time has brought many changes. From Anglo-Saxon times until the sixteenth century, bears, lions, tigers, and wolves had whelps. All versions of the Bible from Wyclif to 1611 used only whelps in such contexts ('as a beare robbed of her whelps in the field', 2 Sam. 17: 8; 'The lion did teare in pieces enough for his whelpes', Nahum 2:12). Cub was first recorded as the name for a young fox in 1530, and, later in the century, by extension, it became the natural term for the young of a bear ('Plucke the yong sucking Cubs from the she Beare', *Merchant of Venice*, 1596), other wild beasts, and the whale. Dogs had whelps until the late sixteenth century. The word puppy (perhaps derived from French *poupée*, doll) had been in use from the fifteenth century onward as a small dog used as a lady's pet, but it was not until the 1590s that it became the regular word for the young of a dog, and not until the 1890s that it came to be applied to the young of a seal and of a shark.

An alphabetical listing of a few of the more exotic names of the young of beasts, birds, and fish gives some hint of the richness of the vocabulary: bachelor (young male fur-seal), elver (eel), eyas (hawk), guga (gannet, in Scotland), joey (kangaroo), and poult (domestic fowl, pheasant, and various game birds).

Of the diminutive suffixes, *-ling* is the most prolific by far, though a good many of them are mere literary effusions of the nineteenth century (antling, doveling, rookling, thrushling, waspling, etc.). It is followed by *-let* (auklet, froglet, swiftlet, wrenlet, etc.). Less often drawn on as suffixes are *-et* (cygnet, hogget, owlet, salmonet, etc., all of them centuries-old words); *-el* (cockerel; pickerel—the young of a pike); *-een* (= the Irish diminutive suffix *-in*) (birdeen; boneen—the young of a pig (Ir. *banbh*, pig)); and *-kin* (lambkin and tigerkin, both non-technical words).

The distribution of the names of the young of the animal kingdom is very uneven. The young of the coal-fish are locally known as podlers, podleys, prinkles, and sillocks. Scartling is a regional Scottish name for the young of a cormorant. In Orkney, Shetland, and thereabouts, scaurie and tarrock are harsh-sounding names given to the young of the common gull. Scrod is one of the names in the USA for a young cod. A widespread name for a young herring or sprat is a brit (or britt). According to the *OED*, a young Arctic whale is called a poggy, and a guinea-pig is a term applied in

Cornwall to the small white cowrie (a gastropod). There are no natural limits to the names given to the young of the animal kingdom.

Sunday Times 4 March 1990

Demotic language

Consider what is happening to the language in its printed form. The following examples are drawn from a wide range of printed sources of the present century: '"Shurrup!" the voice jeered, before anybody else could make a sound' (J. B. Priestley, 1929); 'The plane . . . went down and it fell with a crash in the centre of the garden. "Gotcher!" It was Jiggs' triumphant voice' (Edgar Wallace, 1932); 'But, smatterer fact, I don't like the idea' (V. S. Naipaul, 1957); '"Here have another toffee, Billy." "Orright. Ta."' (J. Wainwright, 1971); 'What she call herself Robin for? Boy's name, innit?' (David Lodge, 1988); '"Zlongazyer gonna redo the walls and floor," suggested the bathroom man, "whydoncha put in a whirlpool bath, a bidet, and a steam shower?"' (*Chicago Sun-Times*, 1990).

Notice the various ways in which the word *yes* is likely to turn up in fiction of the last hundred years: the *OED* has entries for *yaas, yeah, yerse, yip,* and *yup,* variously labelled vulgar, colloquial, non-standard, chiefly US, mainly in Black English, and so on. In the same period the pronoun *you* has moved into new territory in its printed form: the *OED* has entries for *ya, yew, yo, yous(e),* and *yuh,* all it would seem flourishing in one mode of speech or another. Thus: 'Stay off the railroads, they bleed ya dry' (Norman Mailer, 1959); 'Yew wait, young cocky-boy' (Henry Williamson, 1921); 'Niggah, ef'n yo is talkin' tuh me, Ah ain' liss'nin'' (Chester Himes, 1937); 'I want yous two back here at Black Adder' (Xavier Herbert, 1939); 'Yuh bloody secko [= sexual pervert]' (W. Dick, Australian writer, 1969).

Nobody can pretend that the representation of colloquial or non-standard speech is a twentieth-century innovation. But writers, printers, and publishers have sharply increased the percentage of words and phrases that are set down in semi-phonetic form.

It is of interest to see what the modern conventions are, and into what categories they fall. Our century has been particularly productive of new ways of representing exclamations of pain, surprise, wonder, disapproval, etc. These include *ooh* (also *oo, oooah*, etc.), first recorded in 1916: 'It hurts like hell—here . . . I guess my old pump's busted. Ooohh!' (Eugene O'Neill, 1916); 'There was a great "Ooohh" and "Aaahh" as the rocket burst' (Len Deighton, 1964). *Aaahh*, in various spellings, seems to have become much favoured in the last thirty years or so. It now even seems to have acquired a medial -*r*-: 'Enderby . . . writhed in simulated stomach-ache. "Uggggg," said Enderby, "blast it. Arrrrgh."' (Anthony Burgess, 1963); 'A crossword puzzle . . . The clue was "female church head" and the answer was "popess". Aaargh!' (a writer on usage, *Chicago Sun-Times*, 1990). Modern demotic man is becoming keen on sounding his *r*'s, to judge from these examples.

Easily the most significant development in this area of language, however, in the present century is an increase in the use of -*a* (occasionally -*er*) to represent 'of', 'have', or the particle 'to'. All three are shown on a single page of Tom Wolfe's *The Bonfire of the Vanities* (1987): 'But you gotta.' 'You shoulda thoughta that, Irene.' Key words include *outa* (or *outta* or *outer*) = out of (first recorded in the nineteenth century), *sorta* = sort of (eighteenth century), *coulda*, *gonna*, *hafta*, *kinda*, *lotta*, *shoulda*, *useta*, *wanna*, *wanta*, *woulda*, and of course, *loadsamoney*,[1] all products of the last hundred years. Examples lie readily to hand: 'You coulda wanted it to happen' (Bernard Malamud, 1952); 'I'm gonna keep on yelling till you let me out' (Milton Shulman, 1967); 'That little chap must have been really desperate to take that kinda crap' (Caris Davis, 1989); 'Lotta big talk, but when you get there nothin is happenin' (*Black World*, 1971); 'I guess I shoulda knocked' (John Irving, 1978).

Recently Philip Roth, the American novelist, set down the text of an imaginary interview with President George Bush by a journalist. The President is depicted as a person who says 'talkin' and 'somethin' instead of 'talking' and 'something'. He also regularly uses what one might call the *a*-word instead of 'of', 'to', and 'have': e.g. 'the Bill a Rights'; 'I have a kinda dream about this'; 'the how-to we're gonna leave to the states'.

Clearly writers are trying to get to the heart of the informal speech of standard speakers, and also to the grammar and pronunciation of many kinds of non-standard speakers. It is a

---

[1] This expression first came to public attention as a character invented by the comedian and satirist Harry Enfield, and was taken up in May 1988 by Neil Kinnock, the leader of the Labour Party, in a speech attacking the government's policy of encouraging the creation of wealth for its own sake.

healthy trend, no doubt, but there is one casualty. The unerringly accurate ears of young standard speakers hear the reduced form *'ve* (= have) and sometimes translate it wrongly. School essays and family letters abound with examples of the type 'I could of done it', 'You should of heard him'. To which one can only say with Mr Enderby, 'Arrrrgh!'

Sunday Times 6 May 1990

Doubling of consonants with suffixes

There are spelling problems and spelling problems, but one that seems only partially soluble is the question of when to double consonants with suffixes. Anita Brookner in her *Lewis Percy* (1989) has *cossetting*. Maggie Gee, by contrast, in her *Light Years* (1985) has *cosseted*. Nicholas Shakespeare in his *Vision of Elena Silves* (1989) has *ferreted, fidgeted, parroting*, and *uncarpeted*. Andrew Motion in his *Pale Companion* (1989) has *fidgeted* and *rocketed*. Sebastian Faulks, in *The Girl at the 'Lion d'Or'* (1989) has *hiccupped* and *focussing*. I came across *rivetted* in the 28 January issue of the *New Yorker* this year. Half the world writes *benefitted* and the other half *benefited*. The New Zealand writer Barbara Anderson has *caftanned* in her *Girls High* (1991). The American novelist Marilynne Robinson has *nonplused* in her *Housekeeping* (1981). The *OED* lists only *caftaned* and *nonplussed*. In 1964 an American newspaper described the person who abducted a woman with the improbable name of Miss Birdsong as a *kidnaper*. There are areas in which children are *bused* and other areas where they are *bussed* to school. Only one class of words seems to be governed by strict, exceptionless rules—those in which the final *t* is silent (*blue-bereted, crocheting, ricocheting*, etc.). This small class apart, is our language wholly lawless in the matter of doubling? What are our teachers to teach their young?

I can demonstrate that there *are* some rules, and there *are* some groups of words that are for the most part treated differently in Britain and in America. But, as so often, there is a small parcel of words left over that do not respond to legislation. My own guide to such matters is *Hart's Rules for Compositors and Readers at the University Press Oxford* (39th edn., 1983). Americans tend to turn to *The Chicago Manual of Style* (of which I have the 13th edn., 1982, on my shelves).

There is broad agreement about words of one syllable ending with one consonant preceded by one vowel (not counting *u* in *qu*). For such words we double the consonant on adding *-ed*, *-ing*, or *-er*, *-est*, unless it is *w*, *x*, or *y*: thus *beg, begged, begging; clap, clapped, clapping;* but *tow, towed, towing; vex, vexed, vexing; toy, toyed, toying*. The only important exception is that in Britain we normally write *bus, bused, busing* (and *buses*), not the forms with medial *-ss-*. We also write *gases*, but double the consonant in *gassed* and *gassing*.

The trouble really begins with words of more than one syllable. Those that end with one consonant preceded by one vowel double the consonant on adding *-ed*, *-ing*, or *-er*, *-est if the last syllable is stressed* (though not if the consonant is *w*, *x*, or *y*): thus *allot, allotted, allotting; occur, occurred, occurring*, etc.; but *guffaw, guffawed, guffawing; relax, relaxed, relaxing; array, arrayed, arraying*.

Words of this kind *not stressed on the last syllable* do not double the final consonant when inflected. Strict adherence to this rule produces *balloted* and *balloting*, *benefited* and *benefiting*, *biased*, *chirruped*, *filleted*, *gossiped*, *leafleted*, *opened*, *picketed*, *targeted*, *thickened*, *trellised*, *visited*, *vomited*, etc. And, yes, *cosseted* despite Brookner, *caftaned* despite Anderson, and *focused* despite half the writers on both sides of the Atlantic. Major exceptions to the rule in Britain are *inputting*, *outputting*, *worshipped*, and *kidnapped* (together with their derivatives).

Words of more than one syllable ending in *l* fall into a subcategory of their own, and it is in this group that transatlantic differences are most marked. In Britain such words usually show a doubling of the final *l* in inflected forms *whether the last syllable is stressed or not*; thus (last syllable not stressed) *bevelled*, *channelled*, *chiselled*, *counselled*, *grovelled*, *initialled*, *labelled*, *libelled*, *marshalled*, *modelled*, *quarrelled*, *revelled*, *rivalled*, *tunnelled*, etc.; (last syllable stressed) *annulled*, *appalled*, *enrolled*, *extolled*, *impelled*, *instilled*, etc. The doubling rule does not apply when the *l* is preceded by a double vowel or a vowel + consonant, e.g. *ai, ea, ee, oi, ow, ur*, as in *failed, squealed, peeled, boiled, howled, curled*. Another exception is *paralleled, -ing*.

In general, Americans prefer to retain a single *l* in such words: thus *canceled* corresponding to British *cancelled*; and *crueler*, *dialed, dueling, jeweler, labeled, marvelous, traveling*, and so on. Even in this group the parallelism is incomplete, because many

Americans write the uninflected forms of several of the words with a double *l* (*appall, enroll, extoll, instill*, etc.; oddly, they seem not to double the *l* in *annul* or *impel*). And just to complicate things further it is not uncommon to find spellings like *crystallized, imperilled, swivelled*, and *unravelling* in American sources. As I said at the outset, the problem is only partially soluble by the drawing up of rules, but the complications would be reduced somewhat if from now on *everyone* would decide to use only undoubled consonants in *benefited, cosseted, focused, rabbited (on), riveted*, and *targeted*. It's not much to ask.

Sunday Times 9 June 1991

Ellipsis

We think of English as a fairly orderly language of completed sentences, and hardly notice that on occasion and for particular purposes it admits shortenings or ellipses. For example, the spoken language is littered with such phrases as 'Told you so', 'Serves you right', 'Want some?', and 'Sounds fine to me', in each of which a pronoun is dispensed with. We can arrange to call on a person 'at two' when we mean 'at two o'clock'. The spoken form of '1776' is 'seventeen seventy-six' without the words 'hundred and'. Many other such elliptical words, clauses, or sentences exist in everyday English. It is of some interest, I think, to try to determine what kinds of reductive patterns exist in the language and where the boundaries lie.

Ordinary English grammar, in this respect untroubling to native speakers but often causing difficulty to foreigners, actually requires the omission of certain elements: (definite article not repeated) 'He heard the whirr and ∧ click of machinery'; (infinitive marker *to* not repeated before a second infinitive) 'I was forced to leave and ∧ give up my work at the hospital'; (subject not repeated) 'I just pick up wood in a leisurely way, ∧ stack it and ∧ slowly rake the bark into heaps'; (infinitive implied though omitted) 'Knowledge didn't really advance, it only seemed to ∧.' In such circumstances insertion of the omitted elements is not entirely ruled out if some degree of emphasis is required, but in ordinary declarative or narrative prose ellipsis is normal.

While reading Nicholas Shakespeare's *The Vision of Elena Silves* (1989), I collected some examples of slightly more complicated but legitimate types of ellipsis: (various elements understood after the first clause) 'Henriques knew they would eat his tongue for wisdom, ∧ his heart for courage and for fertility ∧ make their women chew his genitals'; (noun replaced by pronoun and then left to be understood) 'He also shared their resignation. He ascribed theirs [= their resignation] to an ability to count to infinity; his [resignation] to the knowledge he was never made for the jungle'; (ellipsis of the adverbial phrase 'of our stuff') ' "They file our stuff in Lima?" "The most interesting ∧." '

There are many other types of ellipsis. Longman's *Comprehensive Grammar of the English Language* (1985) needed more than fifty pages to list, illustrate, and label them all (strict, standard, situational, structural, etc.).

The rule at work is that ellipsis is a process in which certain notional elements may be omitted if they are clearly predictable or recoverable in context. The rule allows for a certain amount of flexibility in the imaginary wording of the understood parts: (adjustment of 'thought' to 'think' after the auxiliary 'didn't') ' "And you thought I was a virgin when I married you?" . . . "No, I didn't" '; (adjustment of 'felt' to 'feel' in the ellipsis) 'She hadn't felt fraudulent about it. Nor had there been any reason to ∧.' The adjustment factor is fractionally higher in T. S. Eliot's 'Several girls have disappeared Unaccountably, and some not able to ∧', but one is predisposed to wrestle slightly more with a literary text than with a non-literary one.

Difficulties arise in certain circumstances, for example, if two auxiliary verbs that operate in different ways are placed together. One cannot say 'No state has or can adopt such measures'. Idiom requires 'has adopted or can adopt such measures'. Fowler permitted the construction 'He is dead, and I not', but I would insist on the insertion of 'am'. When a change of grammatical voice is involved ellipsis spells danger. A reader cannot be expected to make the necessary adjustment from the active voice to the passive and supply an omitted part of the passive form. Fowler's example in *Modern English Usage* will suffice to support the argument: 'Mr Dennett foresees a bright future for Benin if our officials will manage matters conformably with its "customs", as they ought to have been' (insert 'managed').

Comparisons can also produce unacceptable sequences when unwise ellipses are attempted: 'The paintings of Monet are as good or better than those of Van Gogh' (read 'as good *as* or better than').

Again one is reminded that an understood element must be identical with the one that it matches, or at any rate be very closely allied to it.

The unfamiliar ellipses of non-standard English are legion. Writers like Michael Doane and E. L. Doctorow underline the nature of a particular way of speaking among the American underclasses by employing non-standard ellipses in their speech: (omission of 'have') 'Watergate, man. Where you been?'; (omission of 'do' or 'can') 'Well how you expect to get anywhere, how you expect to learn anything?' Such constructions are mostly transparent to standard speakers but instantly mark the speech of the underclasses off from that of people who merely say 'Told you so' and 'Serves you right'. Class barriers are drawn by knowing which elements may safely be omitted in the standard language.

Sunday Times 3 February 1991

Errors

'I am not partiall to infringe our Lawes', declares the Duke of Ephesus in Shakespeare's *Comedie of Errors* (1594). The confusion and errors that ensue in this Christmas revel at Gray's Inn result principally from the coming together of a pair of long-separated twins. Errors and confusions are, of course, not restricted to theatrical comedies. They lie at the very core of our language both in its written and in its spoken form.

First, though, let us recall that the primary sense of the word *error* is that of its Latin original, 'the action of roaming or wandering'. This sense is found in Milton's *Paradise Lost*, 'With mazie error under pendant shades', and in Tennyson's *Gareth and Lynette*, 'The damsel's headlong error thro' the wood'. I suppose it might still turn up in the work of some contemporary poet.

But my concern is with the infringement of linguistic laws, with phrases and sentences that are incorrectly spoken or written through ignorance or inadvertence. Obviously there are errors and errors, ranging from the illiteracy of 'We can't possible know everybodies position' (from an advertisement in a computer journal called *DEC User*, September 1988) to the inadvertent hilarity of 'For Sale—four-poster bed, 101 years old. Perfect for antique lover' (from a report in the American magazine *People*, October 1988).

Schoolteachers derive a great deal of pleasure from the howlers in their pupils' essays. The type is well known: 'Socrates died of an overdose of wedlock. After his death, his career suffered a dramatic decline'; 'The First World War, caused by the assignation of the Arch-Duck by an anarchist, ushered in a new error in the anals of human history.' The linguistic innocence of the young is understandable. It is only when we move into the world of fully adult writing that infringements become reprehensible.

The search for quick headlines is partly to blame. Two American newspapers were responsible for '"Mild" fertility drug produces quadruplets in 3 minutes' (*New Mexican*, Santa Fe, 1981), and 'Sisters reunited after 18 years in checkout line at supermarket' (*Arkansas Democrat*, 1983). But not only headlines. An Associated Press report of the wedding of Sarah Ferguson and Prince Andrew included a brief description of the bridegroom: 'Prince Andrew, 26, the son of Queen Elizabeth and a Royal Navy helicopter pilot.' It is not known whether the reporter is still in the Tower. Perhaps T. S. Eliot should have been clapped in irons for allowing 'staid' (for 'stayed') to appear in the first edition (1939) of *The Family Reunion* ('You have staid in England, yet you seem Like someone who comes from a very long distance'). And the same cell could be made ready for Mr Guy Vanderhaeghe who last year wrote to the *London Review of Books* about barbed wire being '*payed* out from the saddle horn'. One can only imagine the oaths used at the HQ of the *Observer* when it was spotted that the front cover of the 17 April 1988 issue of the magazine presented portraits of eight men under the heading 'The Most Eligible *Batchelors* of 1960'. (An apology was printed in the main section of the paper.)

Lying at the heart of the language is a tendency to confuse like-sounding words. Mrs Malaprop, in Sheridan's *Rivals*, when challenged about her use of 'hard words which she don't understand', protested 'Sure, if I reprehend anything in this world, it is the use of my oracular tongue, and a nice derangement of epitaphs.' She was producing misshapen recollections of the words apprehend, vernacular, arrangement, and epithets. H. W. Fowler believed that such Malapropisms 'pass the bounds of ordinary experience and of the credible'. In his view, Malapropisms normally come as 'single spies, not in battalions, one in an article, perhaps, instead of four in a sentence, and not marked by her bold originality, but monotonously following well beaten tracks'.

He was probably right. Examples of such 'single spies' are not hard to find, though, throughout the English-speaking world. A friend reported hearing a parishioner, who was obviously unfamiliar with the Kiss of Peace formula, turning to her neighbour and saying, instead of 'Peace be with you', 'Pleased to meet you.' Phrases such as 'baited breath' (for bated breath), 'wet the appetite' (whet), and 'hare's breath' (hair's breadth) lie scattered about like broken bottles. Keep the words 'snook', 'intransitive', 'disquieted', and 'recoup' in mind when reading the sentences that follow: 'I'm in no position to cock a snoot at these new acts' (*The Face*, 1986); 'One, a head of English, could not explain the function of an intransigent verb and advised me to "forget it"' (letter to the *Sunday Times*, 1988); 'our man came away profoundly disappointed. And not a little disquietened.' (*Auckland* (NZ) *Star*, 1988); 'No explanation has been given on how investors in the expedition will recuperate the $2.5 million cost of the adventure' (Associated Press report on salvaging relics from the Titanic, 1987). Would that all parts of the English-speaking world were 'not partiall to infringe our Lawes'.

Sunday Times 5 March 1989

Family chronicles at Christmas

We all receive them now—word-processed or cyclostyled or photocopied summaries and descriptions of the intricacies of family life in the year that is coming to an end. In 1988, the ones that reached me happened to come from America, but the custom is much more widespread. The opening formula sets the tone: 'Another year is drawing to a close, and once again we wonder where the time went. This has been a year of ups and downs for us—fortunately, there were more ups than downs.' 'Our personal year has been yet another of abundant pleasure, rich reward, and particular joy.' The pendulum swings this way and that. To judge from the Christmas letters I received, a year of unabated pleasure is a rare thing in family life.

These letters, perhaps mostly the products of middle-aged to elderly parents, tend to lead in with an account of illnesses and anniversaries. These can occur in combination: 'First Jim [*I have changed all names*] got an upper respiratory infection and coughed so hard that he tore some muscles, cracked a rib, and had a lateral hernia! . . . The sad part about this illness was that it kept us from going to Mesa, Arizona, to help Anne's Dad celebrate his 90th birthday.' Or in isolation: 'A knee operation has put an end to squash and I'm endeavouring to replace it with some gym workouts and golf.' Sometimes the detail is a little more intimate: 'Bill entered the hospital in July for an unexpected operation for removal of the prostate gland. His doctor said that Bill had the "granddaddy" of all prostates because his weighed 6 oz. whereas a normal one weighs 1 oz.'

Children are given unqualified praise as they steadily make their way to adulthood. 'Joe's team of four won a nationwide championship in "It's Academic", a quiz game for high school students, and we're understandably proud.' 'Amy remains in her job as the talented and gifted teacher at an elementary public school in Greenwich.' More upmarketly, 'In January we visited older son Jerry and his wife Jodie in Cincinnati and there heard Jerry in a full-length public solo recital at the University . . . His performance of Beethoven's Appassionata Sonata was one of the rich marvels of musical experience.' Blushes are not spared in these semi-private communications. Criticism, if given at all, is expressed with all the venom of a pretended slap on the wrist: 'George has his final exams in three weeks, so he is meant to be swotting but his social life makes that difficult.'

Travel plays a large part in all such chronicles. 'Mary [= the writer] and a woman friend set off for our big adventure to India . . . We travelled by car to Corbett National Park and saw a live tiger while riding an elephant in the jungle . . . While this was going on, Dick [= her husband] went to Turkey and Greece with the local Presbyterian church, "In the Steps of St Paul".'

Some of the annals that reached me commented on political events, especially on the American presidential election and the environment. 'This rural Ohio backwater (from which Bush received 749 votes and Dukakis 2,796) does not shield us from an awareness of the outside world as a source of continuing dismay. We are acutely aware that more than half who voted on 8 November were willing to ignore the mounting shortage of low-cost housing; to ignore our nation's growing mountains of material waste . . .'

Of course health and politics have always formed part of the staple fare of private letters: 'I thank God I am in good case and as good as full whole, both of the fever ague, of mine eye, mine leg, and mine heel, save that I am tender of all these.' (John Paston II to

Margaret Paston, 22 February 1475.) 'People of this country beginneth to wax wild, and it is said here that my Lord of Clarence and the Duke of Suffolk and certain judges with them should come down and sit on such people as be noised [= are rumoured to be] riotous in this country.' (Margaret Paston to John Paston I, 7 January 1462.)

A linguistic curiosity is that the writer normally uses his or her own Christian name instead of the pronoun 'I': 'John's [= the writer's] voluntary teaching has continued into his sixth post-retirement year . . . Ruth [= the writer's wife] continues to be challenged and rewarded by her work as Christian Education Director of our church.' But most of the writers at some point switch back to 'I'.

The signing-off formulas, apart from 'We wish you a Merry Christmas and a Happy New Year', nearly always place emphasis on the same hoped-for things ahead: joy, health, happiness, loving best wishes, prosperity, peace, God's blessing, love. Everyone hopes for nothing less.

Written in March 1989

Future tense

This is a tale about a dead dove, King Harold, and the death of the future tense.

First, the dove. It must have been trapped under the willow tree beside our house. A trail of soft downy feathers began there and ran like a scattering of autumn leaves under the wintersweet and the Michaelmas daisies to a hard gravel-surfaced path. There, in a small heap, slightly disturbed by the wind, lay the main pile of feathers. The bird had died dramatically. The predator (a fox? a cat?) left no flesh, no beak, no claws, only the feathers. That is one kind of death, death in the animal kingdom. The dove, of course, knew about tension, not about the future tense.

Just over 900 years ago King Harold died near Hastings in one of the most famous battles in English history. Before the battle began he doubtless urged his warriors, in resonant Anglo-Saxon, to stand firm and show resolve. He must somehow have brought out that he was talking about the immediate future—the 'future time-reference', as some modern grammarians call it. Had he addressed them in Latin or in Norman French he could have added inflexions to the stem of verbs as clear indicators of the future tense. Harold's own language, our ancestral tongue, lacked such inflexions. There was no distinctive future tense in classical Anglo-Saxon. The present tense served for both.

After the Norman Conquest, *shall* and *will* emerged as the normal auxiliaries for expressing futurity. Malory could write 'I shalle dye a shameful deth' and Wyclif 'Spek thow to vs, and we shulen hear'. The *OED*, with suitable grandeur, sets down all the circumstances in which 'I shall die', and suchlike, came to be thought of as the future tense.

Shakespeare and others exuberantly extended the use of *shall* so that it could also follow *you*: 'If you shall chance to visit Bohemia' (*The Winter's Tale*). As time went on, *shall* continued to be the dominant form in England to express simple futurity but it never became firmly distinguishable from *will* elsewhere. As the *OED* notes, 'to use *will* (instead of *shall*) of events conceived as independent of the speaker's volition is now a mark of Scottish, Irish, provincial, or extra-British idiom'.

A few weeks ago, as I began to busy myself with a reinvestigation of English grammar, I found that some of the traditional rules had been changed. Someone has decided that there is no future tense in English. This is nothing to do with volition or determination nor with the famous cry of 'I will drown and no one shall save me'. Quite simply, grammarians no longer recognize a future tense: 'morphologically English has no future form of the verb in addition to present and past forms' (*A Comprehensive Grammar of the English Language*, edited by Randolph Quirk *et al.*, 1985). At one stroke the future tense has been legislated out of existence. *Will* and *shall*, they say, are 'modals', like *can*, *could*, *may*, and *might*.

Grammar is a living subject (if rarely taught now) and an emotional one. The loss of a tense can of course be 'morphologically' defended; in a curious way it is as if contemporary futureless grammarians were instinctively returning to the time of King Harold. All those centuries ago a king could die in battle knowing nothing of a future tense. To me the sense of loss is close to the anguish I felt over the death of that dove. Death in the afternoon, death of a dove, death of a tense.

Daily Telegraph 24 September 1986

Irregular verbs

Our language has always had a somewhat unstable verbal system and elements of instability still remain. Confirmation of this can be seen whenever we are faced in mid-sentence with the need to use the past tense of verbs like *bet, crow, heave, spin, weave,* and *wet.* An instant choice needs to be made between *bet* and *betted, crew* and *crowed, hove* and *heaved, span* and *spun, weaved* and *wove,* and *wet* and *wetted.* No one would quarrel with the idiomatic flavour of any of the following sentences: 'He burst into her bedroom as the cock crew, or would have crowed, had there been any cocks in Surbiton' (Bernice Rubens, 1987); 'Other families' nurses . . . quailed when we hove in sight' (Penelope Lively, 1987); 'They wove off [on their bicycles] through the theatre crowd' (A. S. Byatt, 1985); 'We spun inland then, to the safest airfield' (Thomas Keneally, 1980). All these examples feel like natural permanent elements of the verbs concerned, yet all have a concertina-like history.

The standard grammar of our time, Longman's *Comprehensive Grammar of the English Language* (1985), declares that there are at present upwards of 250 irregular English verbs, and it divides them into seven main classes with many subdivisions. The irregular verbs are those that depart from the normal pattern of *help* (infinitive), *helped* (past tense), and *helped* (past participle). No one has counted the number of regular verbs like *help* in current English, but they are there in thousands not in hundreds. They all form their past tense in *-ed.* In other words, pastness is indicated by suffixation. By contrast, the irregular verbs indicate past time by various internal changes or variations: *creep/crept, freeze/froze, leave/left, slink/slunk,* and so on.

A great many of the irregular verbs are stable, showing no sign at present of moving over to the majority class or to another of the irregular classes: *become, break, cut, feed, give, go, lose, put, take, teach, write,* and so on. Nothing has come along to disturb them yet. On past patterns, however, it can only be a matter of time before some or even all of them suffer from the buffeting of neighbouring verbs.

If you go back to the beginning of recorded English you find a very different picture. All grammars of Anglo-Saxon lead off with the verbs that indicate their pastness by changes in the root-vowel. These are the so-called 'strong' verbs. Class III of such verbs, for example, contains the verb *helpan* (to help), *healp/halp* (helped, singular), *hulpon* (helped, plural), *holpen* (past participle). Pastness by suffixation affected only some raggle-taggle groups of irregular verbs, and these are called 'weak' verbs.

The transference of large numbers of 'strong' verbs into the 'weak' classes began soon after the Norman Conquest, quickened in the fifteenth century, and was substantially completed by the eighteenth century.

Just to emphasize the unpredictability of it all there has also been some movement the other way—from the so-called 'weak' class to the 'strong' class. Perhaps the best-known of this type is the verb *dig*. Until the later part of the seventeenth century its past tense (and past participle) was overwhelmingly *digged*: 'on all hills that shall be digged with the mattock' (Isaiah (AV) 7: 25); 'two kinsmen digg'd their graves with weeping' (Shakespeare's *Richard II*). The most notable movements of this kind in modern times have affected the verbs *dive*, *sneak*, and *squeeze*.

The past tense *dove* (on the analogy of *drove*) first surfaced in some forms of standard speech in the southern states of America in the nineteenth century. It now turns up quite frequently in American and Canadian sources: 'Forest Hill struck first when Mike Brown dove on a loose ball' (*Toronto Daily Star*, 1970; 'She dove in and rolled onto her back' (*New Yorker*, 1988).

Snuck (meaning 'sneaked') was first noticed in New Orleans a century ago and led a kind of furtive life before it moved out into a wider world: 'Muriel . . . got dressed and snuck out of the house' (Garrison Keillor, 1986); 'happiness snuck up on her like a poacher in the night' (Peter Carey, 1988).

A. A. Milne helped *squoze* (for 'squeezed') into existence: 'He squeezed and he sqoze [*sic*]' (*The House at Pooh Corner*, 1928); he might or might not have been pleased to hear President Reagan use it ('I picked at it and I squoze it and . . . messed myself up a little', 1987).

It is an inescapable fact that all languages are subject to change. But after 800 years of chopping and changing one would be forgiven for thinking that the main battalions of verbs are going to stay put. Who would have thought that there was more to come, or, as the jocular saying goes (and has gone for more than a century), 'who'd a thunk it?'

Sunday Times 20 November 1988

Kaitaia English

The little town of Kaitaia in the subtropical rural north of New Zealand has a daily newspaper called the *Northland Age*. During a recent visit to New Zealand I found that the pages of this newspaper—usually about ten—revealed quite a lot about the nature and quality of provincial New Zealand English in the late 1980s.

Of course the main columns were written in ordinary English sentences, with headlines like 'Teachers strike in children's best interests', 'Clocks back on Sunday', and 'No alternative to prison'. The politics and attitudes of this small citadel of civil rights, if slightly muted, are much as they are in the great cities of the whole of the Western world.

Kaitaia is not, of course, the centre of takeovers and monetarism, hallmarks of the David Lange regime in New Zealand. The glittering effects of 'Rogernomics' (from the name of Mr Roger Douglas, the Minister of Finance) are reflected less in this newspaper than in those in Auckland, Wellington, and the other large cities. Words like 'Coalcorp', 'Electricorp', 'Landcorp', 'Omnicorp', and 'Railcorp', lying like American railway sleepers across the economy of New Zealand, are but distant echoes in Northland.

Metrication is more or less fully in place: 'he was fined $200 with costs of $50'; 'one millimetre or more of rain fell on ten days, with the heaviest fall of 31.0 mm on February 14'. Petrol is sold in litres. Distances are given in kilometres. Curiously though, farm properties were advertised in a mixture of styles: '2000 sq metre section [= building lot], 4 hectares with views', '13 acres of native bush, 2 acres with boat anchorage'.

Not surprisingly, in an area where Maoris form a high proportion of the population, Maori words and phrases were scattered through the pages. In a notice announcing an unveiling of two headstones (a Polynesian custom) it is mentioned that 'Hakari will follow soon after the service'. *Hakari* is a feast. A local club announced that it had put on 'a terrific hangi' (i.e. a Maori-style feast). Birth notices often appeared entirely in Maori.

The vocabulary was decidedly rural and agricultural. Steer calves on sale included familiar British breeds like the Hereford and the Angus, but also many others—'good Simmental cross', 'Maine Anjou cross', and so on. Tourists are invited to visit local woolsheds to watch sheepshearers in action: 'a dinkum Far North attraction'. One firm offered to buy opossum skins. Numerous addresses were of the type 'Beach Road, R.D., Awanui', where R.D. stands for Rural Delivery. The province's ability to produce exotic fruit was underlined by the frequency of references to kiwifruit, tangelos, babacos, nashis, and others.

In one issue a full page was devoted to listing the winners at the Agricultural and Pastoral Show at nearby Mangonui. Women with Christian names like Sherilyn, Norma, Elaine, and Gaye won the passionfruit, pikelets, scones, carrot cake, and bottled fruit sections. 'Girls and boys 16 years and under' called (girls) Brya, Donna, Serena, and Sheree, and (boys) Blair, Darrell, Shane, and Jayden, won various awards in sections devoted to handcrafts, soft toys and arrangements of roadside flowers.

Property advertisements used a combination of local and international terms: 'double basement garage', 'spa pool' or 'whirlpool' (both used for a Jacuzzi), 'games room', 'ensuite', '2 bedroom house plus sleepout', and, mysteriously, 'English style house'. Large areas of land called 'blocks' or 'bush blocks' were up for sale, and some of these contained millable local trees (macrocarpa) or pleasant-looking scrub (manuka).

The apostrophe had a rough time, as it does everywhere: (in a letter to the editor) 'I would like them to remember this fact if something of their's gets stolen'; (in an advertisement) 'Any new referee's or interested persons please attend'.

The crosswords had clues requiring local knowledge: 'a small town in Northland (5)'. More banally, in one, 'American smell' required the answer 'odor' and 'New Zealand smell' the answer 'odour'.

It was hard to come away from this small corner of the English-speaking world—a rural community characterized by weaner pigs, wool bailers, water tanks, mullet bait, boat trailers, and (a recent Antipodean craze) lawns decorated with plastic bottles filled with water which are said to deter passing dogs from leaving their marks—without a feeling that Kaitaia English, like the English used in thousands of other small towns throughout the English-speaking world, is making its independent way forward in a state of protected and guileless linguistic innocence. It is in touch with the Telexed world of Standard English, but at the same time is determinedly going in its own direction without assistance. The price of admission to local social functions is often expressed formulaically as 'Gentlemen $2, ladies a plate', meaning a plate of scones or the like. For half-Kiwi visitors like me the price of linguistic admission to Kaitaia English is the acquisition of an entirely new set of vowels and a wide range of local and Maori vocabulary.

English Today January 1989

Lost language

Of all forms of change, linguistic change is one of the hardest to accept. A country is propped up by its language. Disturbance of the system by the loss of a meaning (for example, the traditional sense of the word *gay*) or by the threatened disappearance of a useful distinction (for example, *disinterested* taking over the territory of *uninterested*) brings more grief, it often seems, than the death of an elderly acquaintance. One is seen as inevitable, the other resistible. The sense of linguistic deprivation is unmistakable.

When you are feeling downcast about the latest disturbances to the language—and of course they are numerous—it is a salutary experience to reread a Victorian classic and re-examine its vocabulary and syntax.

Consider Thackeray's *Vanity Fair*. It was first published in parts in 1847 and 1848. In other words it is less than a century and a half old—in linguistic terms a twinkling of an eye—and yet throughout the novel occur words and constructions that have since vanished altogether or been replaced by other words and usages.

It is partly a matter of technological progress. 'My father's a gentleman, and keeps a carriage,' declares Cuff, the dandy of Dr Swishtail's seminary. The terminology of carriages trundles through the novel like the crunch of coach wheels upon gravel: people 'sit bodkin' (sit wedged in) in 'a light four-inside Trafalgar coach'. They ride in a stanhope, a chair, a brougham, or a barouche. It is a comfortable old-fashioned world. But where are the 'old honest pimple-nosed coachmen' now, and 'the stunted ostler at the inn, with his blue nose and clinking pail'? Indoors, Amelia Sedley, like everyone else, inhabits rooms lit by wax candles and rushlights.

Sir Pitt Crawley had 'taken a strong part' in the 'Negro Emancipation question', but the language of the book is openly racist. Mr Sedley's servant Sambo is always 'black Sambo'. The Revd. Bute Crawley remarks that his brother Rawdon 'looks down upon us country people as so many blackamoors'. Jos Sedley, his

father says, is free to marry Becky Sharp if he wishes: 'Better she
. . . than a black Mrs Sedley, and a dozen of mahogany
grandchildren.' Miss Swartz 'the rich woolly-haired mulatto from
St Kitts', a parlour-boarder at Miss Pinkerton's academy, is not
regarded as eligible by George Osborne: 'I'm not going to marry a
Hottentot Venus.'

Vanity Fair shows off a world of now-abandoned attire (Benjamins,
frock-coats, pantaloons, shovel hats, spencers, ermine tippets),
long-forgotten remedies (James's Powder, Luke Waters, Daffy's
Elixir), and historical drinks (rack punch, rum-shrub). The standard
works referred to are not, of course, Liddell & Scott, the Collins/
Robert French dictionary, and *Brewer's Dictionary of Phrase and
Fable*, but Lemprière, D'Hozier's dictionary, and Mangnall's
Questions.

In an early chapter, almost every day there is a 'frank' (a letter
bearing the superscribed signature of a person entitled to send a
letter post free) from Sir Pitt Crawley to Becky Sharp.

William Dobbin's Latin primer at Dr Swishtail's seminary was
'dogs'-eared', not 'dog-eared'. Dobbin is urged by George Osborne
to come and 'make love to Miss Sharp', but the phrase lacked
sexual suggestiveness. Also without sexual implication is George's
'intercourse' with Amelia in Chapter 17: the meaning is no more
than 'social communication'. 'Ain't' occurs in the conversation of
the servants and also in that of the gentlemen—Sir Pitt Crawley,
Rawdon Crawley, and the two Osbornes. Its by-form 'a'n't' is used
at least once. The past tense and past participle of 'sit' is 'sate'.

French loanwords lie strewn about in a cosmopolitan way, and
not only because the novel is partly set in Belgium. The
predominantly eighteenth-century fashion of adopting French
words in high-level conversation ('casting a *vainqueur* look at Miss
Sharp') was by no means over in the late 1840s.

Words and phrases that are now obsolete or archaic abound: 'the
latter champion was all abroad, as the saying is' (wide of the mark,
astray); 'he served me right' (treated me as I deserved); 'vilipending
the poor innocent girl as the basest and most artful of vixens'
(disparaging).

Thackerary cares about pronouns. Apart from the servants, it is
only Sir Pitt Crawley ('a man who could not spell, and did not care
to read') who gets them wrong: 'Him and his family has been
cheating me on that farm these hundred and fifty years.' The
author remarks: 'Sir Pitt might have said "*he* and his family", to be

sure; but rich baronets do not need to be careful about grammar, as poor governesses must be.'

All the antique words and phrases in *Vanity Fair*, so quickly minted, so rapidly fallen into decline, are listed, like moss-covered gravestones, in the *OED*. For this reason they are not actually 'lost'. But the question remains: which of the disappeared uses would Thackeray himself have deplored the most? The racist language? The old senses of 'make love to' and 'intercourse'? And which do you grieve for yourself? Or is it too soon to grieve over lost Victorian words and enough, really, to mourn uses falling into decline now?

Sunday Times 24 January 1988

Molespeak I

We all know about moles now and the labyrinthine methods they employ.

Orwell's terms *Oldspeak* (Standard English) and *Newspeak* (a sinister artificial language used for official communications), which he used in *Nineteen Eighty-Four* (1949), gave the English-speaking world a new formative element *-speak* denoting 'a particular variety of language or characteristic mode of speaking', as the *OED* has it. They were in due course joined by many others, including *Haigspeak* (duplicitous talk), *airspeak* (unambiguous English used by air traffic controllers), *seaspeak* (similarly unambiguous language now gradually being adopted by mariners), and so on. Apparently *disasterspeak* is the latest type to join the word-family—the kind of Telex English used in time of famine or earthquake to ensure that urgent on-the-spot needs are most advantageously met, e.g. TLX REC-D PLS SEND TENTS NOT PWD-D MILK TKU. This slightly disguised language is child's play, no doubt, compared with what one might call *molespeak*, the deeply obscure linguistic codes and signs used by moles, sleepers, and other elements of the spying trade.

A few years ago I needed to investigate the origin of the word 'mole' in the sense 'a secret intelligence agent who gradually achieves a position deep within the security defences of a country or organization'. John le Carré, to whom I turned for help, replied that as best his recollection served him he 'picked up the word "mole" from the glossary of technical terms appended to the Royal

Commission Report on the Gouzenko case which appeared soon
after the war'. He first used it himself in *Tinker, Tailor, Soldier,
Spy* (1974), but it was not his own invention. I wrote to a
philologist in Leningrad with whom I had corresponded for many
years about Russian loanwords in English, and asked him if the
equivalent Russian word for the small mammal of the family
Talpidae, namely *krot*, was used in Russian for the spying sense.
He was an avid reader, he said, of spy thrillers, but, no, he did not
think that the word 'krot' was used in this way in Russian. Indeed
he almost seemed to be saying that there were no moles in the
KGB.

Meanwhile evidence of various kinds has accumulated. A book
by a writer called Geoffrey Bailey, *The Conspirators* (1960),
declares that in 1935 the Russians recruited a Captain Fedossenko
as a double agent and gave him the alias 'The Mole'.

Some three centuries earlier Francis Bacon, in his *History of the
Reign of Henry VII* (1622), used the word 'mole' in something like
the same way: 'Hee was carefull and liberall to obtaine good
Intelligence from all parts abroad . . . Hee had such Moles
perpetually working and casting to undermine him.' And from
Henry Vaughan's 'The World': 'Yet dig'd the Mole, and lest his
ways be found Workt under ground, Where he did clutch his prey.'

The question is a lexicographical one: who in the present
century first employed the word 'mole' in the counter-intelligence
sense? Perhaps the Ministry of Defence will take up the matter?
And will the KGB let us know whether in fact 'krot' is their word
for this occupation? Perhaps a Telex to the MoD should read
something like this: PLS RPT ORIG OF WD 'MOLE' NEW OED RQRS DTLS
URG. And to the KGB: IS 'KROT' RUSSSPEAK FOR RUSSMOLE PLS TELL
NEW OED ALSO PLS TELL SID BIBI TKU.[1]

Daily Telegraph 24 January 1987

Molespeak II

If you examine Peter Wright's *Spycatcher* for its grammar and
vocabulary what do you find? You have first to ignore the
American spelling (*analyze, caliber, unsavory*, and so on). This
must have been imposed by the American publishers, Viking

---

[1] 'Please tell Sid' was an advertising slogan at the time.

Penguin Inc., since Mr Wright is truly British even though he now lives in Tasmania.

Then you need to be prepared to cope with all those le Carré-ish abbreviations, like SDECE (the French equivalent of MI6) and SF (Special Facility, a phone-tapping device), words like 'cryptonyms', 'intercepts', and 'an illegal', and snappy sentences like 'you'd have to see Six about that'. All very authentic. Or so it would seem.

The author underlines his Britishness when he attacks the 'strangled bureaucratic syntax beloved of Washington officials'. Bill Harvey of the CIA 'explained ponderously that they needed deniable personnel, and improved technical facilities—in Harvey jargon, "delivery mechanisms"'.

But what can one make of the language of the spycatcher himself?

First, the pedantry. He shows a more than ordinary taste for the subjunctive mood ('Terry Guernsey recommended he *talk* to me about a microphone operation') and the possessive gerund ('prior to the *case's* being handed over to Arthur'). The plural of 'Director-General' is pedantically 'Directors-General', not 'Director-Generals', and the plural of 'aide-mémoire' is 'aides-mémoire'. The personal pronouns are carefully controlled. 'Eventually he agreed to allow Hugh Winterborn and *me* to mount an operation.' In such circumstances half the population is now using 'I' instead, more's the pity. He correctly uses the first-person pronoun in 'cleft' sentences like the following: 'It was I who was wrong to raise the issue, not they' ('they', in context, being former members of the Apostles Society in Cambridge).

He eschews 'hopefully' as a sentence adverb, and records the use of such adverbs only in the speech of other spycatchers ('"Intellectually, you simply cannot do this," he [sc. Arthur Martin] burst out in his most precise manner').

Perhaps it was his American publishers who failed to pick up the maladroit inconsistency of 'MI5 *were* living in the past' and 'The CIA *was*, by 1961, the dominant intelligence voice in Washington'. We don't object to a certain amount of variation in such constructions in Britain but the Americans do.

Alas, poor Arthur Martin, one of Peter Wright's most respected colleagues, ignores grammatical concord (though in a thoroughly modern way): '*Someone*,' he said, 'could be running Mitchell as *their* stalking horse.' His 'great flaw was naiveté', says Wright. I wondered if the spycatcher, so punctilious about the details of counterespionage, noticed the controversial nature of Arthur Martin's construction. And then Wright strays himself into using 'fortuitous' to mean 'fortunate'.

Wright's generation was brought up to believe that the splitting of infinitives was simply not done—but, lo and behold, he is so taken by his subject that he splits them all the time ('fears about the ability of the USA to accurately assess Soviet missile capabilities'; 'the CPGB was never again in a position to seriously threaten the safety of the realm'), while sometimes consciously avoiding a split ('if MI5 were finally to get to the bottom of the 1930s conspiracy').

Spycatcher accurately exhibits the uneven grammar of a somewhat elderly conservative speaker (he was born in Chesterfield in 1916), carried away by the excitement of his subject. And his Englishness is partially concealed by the American copy-editors who conducted his book through the press.

Written in August 1987 but not publishable then because Spycatcher *was banned in Britain.*

New words I

According to Sir Ernest Gowers, some missionaries 'of moral uplift' adopted as their slogan 'Prayerize, Picturize, Actualize'. He greatly doubted if this formula would help them very much in the practice of meditation. He meant, of course, that no good can come of any new word ending in *-ize*. Nevertheless, quite a few new formations of the same type continue to fall through this hated grill, among the latest being *condomize* (also *condomania*), *entitize*, and *incentivize* (I leave readers to work them out for themselves).

The arrival of a copy of *The Random House Dictionary of the English Language*, Second Edition, Unabridged (published in America towards the end of 1987) prompts me to give an account of some of the new words that are pushing and shoving their way into the language. The publishers of the dictionary say that it has 315,000 entries in its 2,500 pages, and of these 50,000 are said to be 'new words'. There are also said to be 75,000 new meanings. There is no particular reason to question the figures. Nobody doubts the fecundity of the language. It is mildly curious, though, that none of the words just mentioned—I have noted them down in the last few months from quite respectable sources—appears in the *RHD*.

It is self-evident that many of the new words come from the new technology (e.g. *front-end processor*) and others from politics. An American politician called Howard Phillips opposed last year's INF treaty and said that 'we must defeat the *Reagachev* Doctrine'. A new word was (temporarily) born.

Naturally none of us is likely to know, or even to encounter, all these new words. We must wait for the lexicographers to collect them for us. In practice the great majority of us spend our lives eking out the words that we acquired by the age of about 25. Later we add a word here, and drop one there, pushed about by fashion and by the vicissitudes of life and work, but we get by with a more or less constant number of words that we actively understand and use. The exact number varies from person to person, but it can be assumed that the figure is lower than the number of words used by Shakespeare (a little over 30,000).

From various sources I have hunted down some other new words (not all of them listed in the *RHD*). The first group (with date of first record where known) belongs to the slightly farcical world of blends and shortenings. They include *arb* (1983, short for 'risk arbitrageur', a professional risk dealer on the Stock Exchange); *bluesical* (a blend of 'blues' and 'musical'); *cafetorium* (a large room, especially in a school, used both as a cafeteria and an auditorium); *ditsy* (1978, conceited, fussy, etc.); and *elevonic* ('elevonic elevators have microprocessor controls that use computerized information to make the elevator system smarter in terms of knowing where to pick people up, etc.'). Such coinages are very fashionable now. Nobody seems to mind them very much. They are not much loved, but then they are not exactly unloved either.

Unobjectionable too are relatively recent words like *adversarial* (1970), *aerobics* (1968), *bar code* (1963), *beta-blocker* (1970), *break-dancing* (1982), *cardphone* (1978), and *cash dispenser* (1967). They reflect small breakthroughs in society. They are, if you like, 'user-friendly' words (itself a new word of the 1970s).

Even some of the new words for horrid concepts or conditions— *Aids*, *battered wife*, *child abuse*, and *nuclear winter*, all of which have emerged in the last decade—are unexceptionable as words.

The slang of the 1980s contains a few quite pleasing bin-liners: *bonk* (1975; 'I cannot find *bonk* in my dictionary', Boris Becker), *brill* (1981, brilliant), and *eighty-six* (= no longer on the menu;

used in America since the 1930s). Does anyone object to such novelties?

But not everything in the garden is rosy. Bernard Levin recently (and with justification) lashed out at the language used by some of the bureaucrats in one of the London boroughs. An MEP complained on Radio 4 about the 'obscuranto' used in many EEC reports. None of us likes, or sees any justification for, such bafflegab.

The makers of new words, like politicians, need to win the hearts and minds of the general public. The Labour Party, despite what was widely regarded as a good campaign, failed to win the election last year. Many of the new words will need more than a good campaign to survive. If you are a betting person how much money would you be prepared to place on the following newish words: *adamance* (state of being adamant), *bazooms* (breasts), and the rash of new words ending in *-tainment* among them *infotainment* (serious news presented as entertainment), *docutainment*, and *edutainment*?

Sunday Times 3 April 1988

New Words II

Anyone familiar with the American publications *The Barnhart Dictionary Companion* and *American Speech* will know that the world is full of scholars busily gathering up new words and meanings as soon as they are formed or come into prominence. Such journals give evidence of the first recorded use of neologisms, as well as other illustrative examples drawn from relevant sources. A definition is generally also provided, and details of the etymology and pronunciation of the new words.

This fodder is then subjected to various tests and trials by lexicographers in the great dictionary houses, merged with material they have collected independently, and a proportion of the new uses—varying according to the size of the dictionary—make their way into the dictionaries of the English-speaking world.

As an indication of the rate of entry of new words and meanings into the language, the latest issue of the quarterly *Barnhart Dictionary Companion* gives details of more than 200 separate items. It begins with the medical abbreviation *ABC* (airway, breathing, and circulation) and ends with *windshield appraisal* (a brief, superficial inspection of collateral by a lender, especially of the house of an applicant for a home-equity loan). The main classes of words listed include acronyms like *CAMOS* (computer-aided mapping of sonar, which is used in the production of three-dimensional maps); a rash of words with the scandal-suggestive suffix *-gate* of 'Watergate' (*cookiegate, copygate, harborgate, sewergate*, etc.); and mind-aching amalgamations like *compunications* (from *computer + communications*), *sparticle* (the first *s* of *supersymmetry + particle*), and *warnography* (gruesome films, from *war + (por)nography*). The longest word is *videoteleconferencing* (the holding of a conference among a group of people linked by telephone and video display); and the most amusing is *Twinkie defense*, a legal defense (I retain the American spelling), especially for murder, which attributes the aberrant behaviour and impaired mental competence of the accused to his or her diet of junk food ('Twinkies' are cream-filled cup-cakes).

As one would expect, most of the new words are drawn from areas of life made familiar to us all by the media: drugs, pollution, surrogacy, terrorism, high finance, computers, and the busy, often word-insensitive, pens of scientists and technologists.

Some of the words attain virtually instant recognition—words like *enterprise zone, Hezbollah* (Children of God), *ozone hole*, and *safe sex*—though time will tell how enterprising, Godlike, perforated, and safe the concepts will prove to be.

The trading markets of the world have come up with *harakiri swap* (a trade of currency which yields a loss or very little profit). From the laboratories comes *squark*, yet another kind of quark. The world of social welfare has produced *motel children*, a term used in some parts of America for children of families living in motels and supported by welfare programmes.

One cannot compete, at least in quantity, with the institutional gatherers of new words and meanings, but some that have come my way may be of general interest. The United States still leads the way, though a good many of the words slip into some kind of currency here in the up-market weeklies and in trendy magazines aimed at the young. From the name of Robert Bork, a former US Court of Appeals judge who was nominated for the Supreme Court but whose appointment was disallowed by the Senate Judiciary Committee, has come the verb *bork* meaning 'to oust', a coinage of the present year. The word *bumfuzzled* (confused), which has lurked in American regional speech for almost a century, has recently inched into more general use ('The bumfuzzled police chief, a former New York homicide detective, said: "I wouldn't mind having this guy [an escapologist] in my burglary unit."'— *Chicago Tribune*, 1988). *Celebutantes* now stalk the entertainment world: 'a series of bruising encounters with gentlemen of the press has taught the Hollywood celebutante Brigitte Neilsen that the art of self-preservation starts with . . . camouflage' (*Melody Maker*, 1988). The latest American word for a stupid or ineffectual person (competing with *nerd*) is *dork*: 'shambly dorks seem surprisingly reticent to warm to Aztec Camera's more recent excursions' (*Melody Maker*, 1988). It has already produced an adjective, *dorky*: 'She asked Kate what she thought of Cle. "He's dorky," Kate responded. She said she didn't like his glasses' (*Chicago Tribune*, 1988).

The manufacturing process will doubtless continue. Never before has it been so clear that spare-part words are lying about ready to use: elements like *-henge*, as in *Carhenge*, a monument of old cars set upright in the ground to resemble Stonehenge; and even *Spudhenge*, a monument of potatoes displayed Stonehenge-like in a recent *New Yorker* cartoon; and *fink* (an American word for a contemptible person), as in *finkography*, a kiss-and-tell biography written by former governmental officials like Larry Speakes or Donald Regan. Some will say we could well do without these leaden gifts from an all-too-fertile world. Maybe it's all the fault of junk food and the concept of Twinkie defense.

Sunday Times 18 September 1988

New Words III

One of the pleasures of lexicography is the pursuit and gathering up of unregistered words. The second edition of the *OED*, published earlier this year (1989), included some 5,000 previously unrecorded words and meanings. Some were the kind you would expect—*acid rain*, *Aid* (as in *Band Aid*, *Live Aid*, etc.), *glasnost* and *perestroika* (two words which, like Laurel and Hardy, seem always to occur together), *workaholic*, and so on. Others were less familiar, e.g. *buzkashi* (pronounced bush-ka-shee, with stress on the final syllable), an Afghan sport played by teams on horseback competing for the carcass of a goat, and *greymail* (US *graymail*), a threat by the defence, especially in a spy trial, to expose government secrets unless charges are dropped.

The Longman Register of New Words, also published this year, produced its own, somewhat more modest trawl. The new words ran from *ableism* (unfair discrimination in favour of able-bodied people) to *zootique* (a landscaped zoo designed so that the animals are placed in habitats approximating as closely as possible to their natural ones).

Such is the fecundity of the language, however, that any diligent private collector can fill a basket with new words and meanings that have not yet made their way into dictionaries. Some of them of course are likely to be ephemeral—formations, for example, like *mythconception* (a punning word coined with reference to some misconceptions about Israel's policy towards the Arabs) and *threepeat* (a third playing of a musical performance, etc.). Headline writers 'outawfulled' (itself a new word) these by slapping the words *pignap* and *rabbitnap* above stories about the theft of pigs and rabbits. The American presidential election brought into daily use the expressions *sound bite* (brusque one-liners like Lloyd Bentsen's to Dan Quayle, 'Senator, you're no Jack Kennedy') and *spin doctor* (this one in the *Longman Register*), a person who gives a slant (or 'spin') to a proposal, policy, etc.

A new generation of naturalistic paintings came to be called *Artoons*. A chemical called *Alar* (alias daminozide), a growth regulator used on apples to promote firmness, joined the ranks of environmentally unfriendly substances, along with CFCs and PCBs (we are all half-educated now in the threats to the environment).

The car wash is out in large cities in the USA. If you want your car cleaned, you can now take it to an *automotive appearance center*. If any part needs to be repaired or replaced, you take the car to an *automotive aftermarket car center—auto mall* for short—a very large (up to 50,000 square feet) multi-purpose servicing building. 'Customers want convenience and speed,' an auto mall spokesman said recently. 'In some of them the franchise owners even include sushi bars and dance studios, spots that give customers a place to keep busy while their cars are being serviced.'

At least in the Chicago area, a new form of hamburger called a *slider* was launched by the White Castle chain. The beef is cooked on a griddle over a layer of onions, and the result is said to be delicious by those who like that sort of thing. The *Sunday Times* gave coverage to *Callanetics*, an exercise programme devised by the American fitness guru Callan Pinkney. A device called a

CAIVman (= Computer Audio Interactive Video Manipulator), a hand-held multimedia disc player, reached the drawing-board stage, and will shortly be used in schools 'to access video images, sound track, and text', for example, they said, the minute-by-minute activities inside a Space Shuttle. John le Carré, in his novel *The Russia House*, wrote about *espiocrats*, the governors of the intelligence service.

Most of the 'enrichment' of the language seems to be happening in the United States or even in mid-Atlantic. The *Jason robot* enabled deep-sea divers to explore the wrecked remains of the *Titanic*. Felice Schwartz, the president of Catalyst, a women's business-research group, stirred up controversy by suggesting in the *Harvard Business Review* the concept of the *mommy track*, describing the middle-speed track designed for career women who realize that they cannot reach the fast track of top management without causing some emotional deprivation to their children. American feminists were enraged.

The *Chicago Tribune* of 9 August reported that 'George Bush, James Bond and drug king-pins all smoke the same waters with Cigarette boats.' Cigarette boats? Speedboats, apparently first named after a prohibition-era sailing vessel that ran bootleg rum and tobacco from the Caribbean islands to the USA. President Bush uses his Cigarette boat *Fidelity* to head out to where the bluefish are biting. He took President Mitterand for a ride in it.

Perhaps the most chilling new word of the year is the expression 'go wilding', a term used to describe attacks made by 'wolf packs' of youths on joggers and cyclists in Central Park, New York. The vocabulary of violence is never exhausted.

Sunday Times 3 December 1989

The prefix *a-*

To judge from Peter Carey's novel *Oscar and Lucinda* (1988), the prefix *a-* is vibrantly alive and well: 'the whole place a-clatter with hooves and rolling iron'; 'Oscar had imagined a small pink nose all aquiver'; '"Is your mistress at home?" He was informed she was still abed.' It does not take long to establish that other modern writers are equally interested in words of this type: 'I always used to go through the town with my nose a-quiver like a dog's' (Gerald Durrell, 1988); 'Tup was at the door, face all a-grin with crooked teeth' (Maurice Gee, 1987); 'He damped her forehead as she lay abed' (Bernice Rubens, 1987); 'He's literally atremble with sensibility' (*New Yorker*, 1987); 'The Royal Ascot races . . . are agaggle with gossip' (*Chicago Sun-Times*, 1989).

The *OED* lists fifteen distinct uses of the prefix *a-*, some of them in abeyance, some in restricted use, all of them absorbing. This is number two. It is a worn-down version of the Anglo-Saxon preposition *on*, but after the Norman Conquest and ever since has been seen as a prefix attachable to certain elements with the senses 'in', 'on', 'engaged in', or 'at'. Some of the formations of this type are of long standing in the language: *abed, afield, afire, alive, asleep*, for example, go right back to the Middle Ages. Others, like *askew, astoop, aswim*, and *aweary* are first caught sight of in the sixteenth and seventeenth centuries.

Shakespeare's plays provide plenty of evidence of the fecundity of the prefix, though, to judge from the Oxford original-spelling edition of his works, the Bard regarded the 'a' as a detached element, a quasi-preposition perhaps, as it normally stands separate from the following word: 'And Gentlemen in England, now a bed, Shall thinke themselues accurst they were not here' (*Henry V*); 'Poore Tom's a cold' (*King Lear*); 'How now prince Troylus, wherefore not a field' (*Troilus and Cressida*).

The evidence in the *OED* suggests that the most substantial new wave of such formations came in literary works of the nineteenth century. Newly minted words beginning with *a-* lie strewn around like fallen apples: 'Had the flowers shrunk, the warm breeze grown a-chill' (William Morris, 1870); 'The lion of Venice with brows a-frown' (Joaquin Miller, 1878); 'He throws himself all a-sprawl upon the ground' (Richard Jefferies, 1878); 'On some broad stream, with long green weeds a-sway' (William Morris, 1858). Elizabeth Barrett Browning could not resist them. In 'Aurora Leigh' (1856) alone, one finds: 'The dark a-mutter round him'; 'My hands a-tremble'; 'As a dog a-watch for his master's foot'. She was not alone: 'All asmear with filth and fat' (Dickens, 1861); 'So blackens a brand . . . asmoulder awhile from the fire' (Swinburne, 1880).

It is noteworthy that some of the formations of this type are the equivalent of participial forms in *-ing* or *-ed* (*a-grin* = grinning, *a-tremble* = trembling, *a-smear* = smeared, etc.), while in others the prefix is more prepositional in nature (*abed, afield*, etc.).

The fourteenth of the fifteen types accounts for a wad of words derived ultimately from Greek ἀ- (before a consonant) or ἀν- (before a vowel) + a following element. The prefix is the Greek equivalent of 'without', 'not', or '-less'. Many such words are now regarded by speakers as not containing a prefix at all, since the initial 'a' has totally fused with what follows. Thus *abyss* is scarcely recognizable as answerable to the Greek adjective ἄβυσσος without bottom, bottomless, i.e. as a combination of the privative element ἀ- 'without' and βυσσος 'depth of the sea'. Even more so, *amethyst* has moved a long way from its starting-point, Greek ἀμέθυστος λίθος 'unintoxicating' stone, from the notion that an amethyst was a preventive of intoxication. The passage of time inevitably obscures the origin of many words.

More transparent uses of this negative or privative prefix *a-* are found in two main groups of English words: (*a*) terms of the arts or sciences having Greek bases, but normally coming into English through medieval or modern Latin, as *abranchiate* (having no gills, first recorded 1855), *acatalectic* (not wanting a syllable in the last foot, complete in its syllables, 1589), *anaesthesia* (absence of sensation, 1721), *anorexia* (want of appetite, 1598), and *apetalous* (without petals, 1706); (*b*) words formed in the nineteenth century on Greek elements, as *agnostic* (1870), *aseptic* (non-putrescent, 1859), and *asexual* (used of certain plants, 1830).

In the last century or so, privative *a-*, most commonly now pronounced with the same sound as the 'ay' in 'say', has also come to be attached to a limited number of adjectives in general use, as *ahistoric* (1937), *ahistorical* (1957), *amoral* (1892), *apolitical* (1952), *asexual* (applied to people, 1896), *asocial* (1883), and *atypical* (1885), and to their derivatives (*amorality*, etc.). But this fourteenth use of *a-* is not applicable to most adjectives. We can say curious, incurious, non-curious, and even uncurious, but not acurious.

Sunday Times 6 August 1989

Punctuation: apostrophes

Who has not seen the likes of the following: 'The class lead was their's by Liverpool, where they were 20th overall' (*Rally Sport*, 1987); 'The right candidate will be a competent typist familiar with Word Processor's and VAT returns' (*Reading Chronicle*, 1987); 'Movie's' (sign in a video shop in Abingdon, Oxfordshire, 1987); 'The label of the year, Def Jam, confirmed it's dominant position' (*The Face*, 1988); 'Who's attitudes need to change?' (*Times*

Educational Supplement, 1986); 'Be a Detective: Whose been in the woods today?' (South Oxfordshire Countryside Education Trust leaflet, 1986)?

The *Chicago Tribune* recently reported that every now and then 'a college professor will rise up out of the tranquil academic sea and beseech the Almighty or the faculty committee to do something about the apostrophe'. One professor claimed to have inserted at least 50,000 apostrophes in the written work of his students in a single semester, and to have moved or removed a similar number. Ask any schoolteacher here and the response is much the same.

But if anyone should think that the misuse of apostrophes is a new phenomenon, just take a look at the following comments made by Henry Alford, Dean of Canterbury, in his book *The Queen's English* (1864): 'There seems to be some doubt occasionally felt about the apostrophe which marks the genitive case singular. One not uncommonly sees outside an inn, that "*fly's*" and "*gig's*" are to be let. In country town blessed with more than one railway, I have seen an omnibus with "RAILWAY STATION'S" painted in emblazonry on its side.'

A century before Alford, the polymath Joseph Priestley, discoverer of oxygen, philosopher, radical politician, and grammarian, remarked in a mild-mannered way in his *Rudiments of English Grammar* (1761): 'Sometimes we find an apostrophe used in the plural number, when the noun ends in a vowel; as in *inamorato's, toga's, tunica's, Otho's, a set of virtuoso's*'. He took these from the works of Addison.

In the two centuries since Priestley, what seems to have happened is that gentle observations about the type *grotto's/ tomato's/video's* have turned into shouts of anguish. How *could* they do this to us, is the prevalent view.

There are marginal cases, of course, as there always are. In certain circumstances it is permissible, though never obligatory, to insert an apostrophe as part of the plural marker. Thus publishing houses vary widely in their use or non-use of the apostrophe in the plural of letters (*POW's; mind your p's and q's; concentrate on the three R's*), numbers (*the 1960's*); and words that are being discussed (*there are too many if's and but's*).

Back to the possessive case. Standard examples are (1) With the apostrophe preceding the *s* as a sign of the singular: *an hour's drive, the British Wildlife Appeal's slogan, a friend of Picasso's, in a week or so's time*. (2) With the apostrophe following the *s* as a sign of the plural: *ten days' holiday, the major civil servants' unions, the pit ponies' stalls.*

If life were simple the matter would end there. Sharp division of opinion occurs about the plural of words or names ending in a sibilant or, in foreign names, ending in a silent *-s* or *-x* (*Rabelais, Le Roux*). Usage guides offer finely drawn verdicts. For example, OUP's *Hart's Rules* favours *Charles's, Hicks's, St James's Square*, but for ancient names, *Ceres' rites* and *Xerxes' fleet*. It also recommends *Rabelais's* (pronounced as three syllables) and *Le Roux's* (two syllables). It further recommends omission of a final *-s* when the last syllable of a name is pronounced *-iz*, as in *Bridges'* (not *Bridges's*) and *Moses'*. In other guides, other recommendations. Place-names and some other names exhibit both styles: thus *Land's End, St John's Wood* (London), *St Michael's Mount* (Cornwall); but *All Souls College* (Oxford), *Earls Court, St Neots* (Cambridgeshire).

A primary cause of uncertainty about the positioning of the possessive apostrophe is the fact that the apostrophe has another function altogether, namely its use as a sign of elision, especially in reduced forms of 'is' (*it's time to move on*), 'has' (*I wonder where John's got to*), and 'us' (*Let's go home now*). It is this doubling of functions that leads to the grammatical morass of *it's* and *its*, *who's* and *whose, they're* and *their*, and all the rest.

Sunday Times 4 December 1988

Punctuation: hyphens

If we are to believe H. W. Fowler, 'The chaos prevailing among writers or printers or both regarding the use of hyphens is discreditable to English education' (*Modern English Usage*, 1926). His account of the main hyphening sins—note that he used 'hyphen' as a verb not 'hyphenate', and so do I—took up eleven columns of his celebrated book. His aim was to demonstrate that 'the wrong use or wrong non-use of hyphens makes the words, if strictly interpreted, mean something different from what the writers intended'. His examples included 'a superfluous hair-remover (i.e. a hair-remover that no-one wants)', and 'the Acting-British Consul at Shiraz (i.e. the Consul who was pretending to be British)'. Clearly such examples of lazy writing or negligent proofreading should be frowned on. He went on to classify the main types of hyphens in their various groups. In passing he distinguished the type 'holding a red-hot poker' (in which 'red-hot' is a compound adjective in the attributive position) from 'holding a red hot poker' (in which a red-coloured poker is hot). He also distinguished the phrasal verb 'to put up' (no hyphen) from 'a put-up job', where a hyphen is needed. Throughout the article he insisted that 'the hyphen is not an ornament' but must earn its keep. There is much in the article of permanent value.

Time has moved on and new habits have emerged. Our language, or that variety of it used in management reports, seems to be slowly making its way towards the acceptance of German-type chains of words. Witness such phrases as 'a grammar-based database management system' and 'fast string searching capabilities' in a recent Canadian report on an ambitious computer project. Obviously we are not yet ready to print the second of these as 'faststringsearchingcapabilities', but that would appear to be the long-term destination of multiple-element phrases in management reports. In fact a hyphen in 'string-searching' would have helped a layman to see which word belonged with which, but in general it is as well to keep as many words apart as possible in such technical reports. The recipients will understand. The compiler of a Mobil Report in 1987 did well to leave the following sentence unhyphened: 'Margins benefited from favourable netback crude purchase agreements.' After a pause for reflection, the meaning of this five-unit phrase is apparent enough. So too are the unhyphened elements in 'the undisputed Secret Service crossword king' in a recent book about spies.

A correspondent has prevailed upon me to make a formal investigation of a class of hyphens, now printed, he thought, pretty well everywhere. He objected to 'the extraordinary prevalence of unnecessarily hyphenated compound adjectives of the type "newly-discovered" and "recently-reported"'. The results of my investigation were not exactly what I had expected.

As it happened I had been collecting evidence for this very class of words for the last eighteen months or so, but I had not analysed it into groups. Nor had I turned to the *OED* to see what it had to offer.

Under several headwords, the *OED* insists that an adverb like 'partly' is 'usually hyphened to a participial adjective when preceding its substantive'. Illustrative examples are then provided from three nineteenth-century sources, including Thomas Hardy,

for 'partly-closed', 'partly-heard', and 'partly-paid'. There are
similar notes in the *OED* under 'dearly', 'highly', 'newly', 'poorly',
'recently', and some other adverbs. The statements are supported
by numerous illustrative examples from 1590 onwards, e.g. 'His
newly-budded pinions to assay'—Spenser, 1590; 'his dearly-loved
mate'—Milton, 1625; 'some lightly-budding philosophers'—Ruskin,
1860; 'highly-integrated freight services'—*Jane's Freight Containers*, 1969.

The Dictionary is clearly claiming that adverbs ending in *-ly*
followed by a past or present participial adjective normally require
a hyphen *if they are immediately followed by a noun*. If they are
not followed by a noun, that is, are in some other position in the
sentence, no hyphen is required. Secondly the evidence in the *OED*
pointed to the fact that a hyphen was very rarely used (and probably
should not be used) when the element between the *-ly* adverb and
the noun is a simple adjective.

My own corpus of evidence from English language sources of the
1980s has a substantial number of sentences of the type 'we invent
scientific theories . . . to make it intellectually respectable'. None
is hyphened. On the other hand, a quarter, but only a quarter, of
examples in the attributive position were hyphened ('finely-
decorated buildings', 'lawfully-elected prime ministers'). Three-
quarters of the examples were left unhyphened ('deeply indoctrinated
anthropologists', 'childishly crayoned violets'). When the middle
element is an ordinary adjective ('an extremely hot day', 'a
famously unanswerable question') a hyphen is hardly ever used.

The *OED*'s preference for this class of words was doubtless right
for the 1880s. A century later the advice I offer to writers and
printers is to omit the hyphen altogether and print, for example,
'some recently acquired private press material' and 'a statistically
significant relationship'. You will be in good company: the
Bodleian Library and the Oxford University Press.

Sunday Times 15 May 1988

Repetition

Chance repetition of words is a natural feature of the language.
Sometimes it happens because the repeated words are just part of
the ordinary way in which verbs work: 'Of course he too had had a
choice, and still had one' (Iris Murdoch, 1989); 'The way in which

we do do such things' (BBC Radio 4, 1990). At other times it occurs because the same word is used twice with different functions: 'The heart wasn't beating . . . Whoever he was, the chap had had it' (Michael Innes, 1956); 'She brings with her her daughter Elizabeth-Jane' (Margaret Drabble, 1985); 'such publicity as there was was left to the chairman and senior editors' (Philip Howard, 1990); 'None has been seen by a consultant, and that in K has not been looked at at all' (private letter, 1990).

The phenomenon is not new: 'Harry could forgive her her birth' (George Meredith, 1861). Nor, of course, is it restricted to the English of this country: 'the front page [of the newspaper] was missing and all there was was columnists and the life-style section' (Garrison Keillor, 1990).

Any awkwardness residing in such repetitions is normally passed over as something that is inevitable and unavoidable. If there is any question of loss of clarity a comma is inserted between the repeated words: 'And while we're at it, it wasn't me with the fedora at Bea's sweet-sixteen' (Mordecai Richler, 1980). In spoken English, in such slightly convoluted circumstances, a pause is inserted between the repeated words: 'We are getting people who had a right to be out [*pause*] out' (William Waldegrave, BBC 1 News, 1990).

Jespersen's *Modern English Grammar* draws attention to a spectacular example of word repetition in Addison's *Spectator* (May, 1711). In reply to an article about the increasing use of 'that' for 'which' in the early eighteenth century, a pseudonymous writer called 'That' submitted an ironic reply: 'My lords! with humble submission, *That that* I say is this: *that that that that* gentleman has advanced, is not *that, that* he should have said to your Lordships.' It takes a little working out but the meaning comes through.

Back to the twentieth century. Common or garden repetition has been joined in quite recent times by a remarkable domino-type repetition of 'is'. It occurs only in spoken English, and principally in sentences beginning with 'The problem is', 'The question is', and similar phrases.

An American scholar, Dwight Bolinger, first consciously noticed the reduplicated use of 'is' in a speech by a former president of the Linguistic Society of America in 1971: 'My real feeling is, is that there is . . .' This example could, I suppose, have been the result of a momentary hestitation. But Bolinger, by then alerted to the construction, noted that it was breaking out everywhere, mostly in radio or television broadcasts, often with no perceptible pause between first and second uses of 'is'; e.g. 'The problem is, is that . . .' (a Californian radio station, 1978); 'The other problem is is on the demand side' (as against the supply side) (ditto, 1985). Sometimes the repetition is disguised or deflected by a change of tense: 'The strange thing was, is that . . .' (1981); 'Some of the problems in loading the structure was is that . . .' (1985).

I was beginning to dismiss it as an idiosyncratic American use, when a correspondent from West Yorkshire, Mr James A. Porter, wrote to say that he had encountered this weird type of construction on the BBC 'scores of times': e.g. 'The question is, is if the merger goes ahead, will . . .?' (David Owen, BBC, 30 August 1987); 'What is clear is this, is what the Labour Party intend to do will lead to . . .' (Nigel Lawson, BBC, 26 May 1987); 'But isn't that the problem, is that . . .' (BBC Radio 4 on a radio call-in with Nick Ross, 6 November 1990).

I began to watch out for examples myself and was soon rewarded: 'The curious thing about it is that, is . . .' (Peter Barnes, BBC 1, 29 July 1990); 'My message is to the government, is . . .' (Gerald Kaufman, BBC 1, 25 August 1990). Somehow the construction had crossed the Atlantic in the mysterious way in which such things happen.

The pleonastic doubling or repetition of 'is' is clearly a marked feature of modern spoken English. A copytaker setting down an example of the use would normally, I think, insert a comma between the two occurrences or silently omit the second 'is' as being otiose or 'a mistake'. In the examples I heard myself there was no perceptible pause before the second occurrence. Contextually the construction seems to be just some kind of unguarded syntactic stuttering. Or perhaps it is an example of some deep-structured linguistic domino effect?

Sunday Times 14 October 1990

Sentence adverbs

In an August issue of *The Times*, coastguard Peter Legg, senior watch officer at Dover, was reported as saying 'Frankly we don't want them.' He was referring to Channel swimmers and the hazard they present to shipping in the world's busiest waterway. His use of 'frankly', with ellipsis of 'to speak', draws attention to one of the most bitterly contested of all the linguistic battles that are being fought out in the last decades of the present century.

An unofficial war against certain uses of adverbs ending in *-ly* broke out in the late 1960s. On a visit to New York in 1968 I was met at JFK Airport by an OUP publisher. 'Keep your head down about "hopefully",' he told me. 'Half the world is using it and everyone else is hating it.' It quickly emerged that 'hopefully' was regarded as acceptable when it meant 'in a hopeful manner', as in 'to set to work hopefully', but not acceptable when used to mean 'it is hoped (that), let us hope', as in 'We asked her when she expected to move into her new apartment, and she answered, "Hopefully on Tuesday".' A little more than two decades later the unofficial war rumbles on. It has divided communities and threatened friendships. A resolution does not seem to be immediately at hand.

Let me state a general proposition: in the twentieth century there has been a swift and immoderate increase in the currency of *-ly* adverbs used to qualify a predication or assertion as a whole. The *-ly* adverbs concerned include *actually, basically, frankly, hopefully, regretfully, strictly,* and *thankfully.* Suddenly, round about 1968, and with unprecedented venom, a dunce's cap was placed on the head of anyone who used just one of them— *hopefully*—as a sentence adverb.

The simplest type of *-ly* sentence adverb is one that begins a sentence and is marked off from what follows by a comma: 'Unhappily, there are times when violence is the only way in which justice can be secured' (in which 'Unhappily' = it is an unhappy fact that); 'Agreeably, he asked me my name and where I lived' (= in a manner that was agreeable to me); 'Frankly, I do not wish to stop them' (= in all frankness, to speak frankly); 'Well, that won't happen at Pringle's, hopefully as they say. Hopefully.' (= it is to be hoped). These examples are drawn, respectively, from T. S. Eliot's *Murder in the Cathedral* (1935), a 1987 issue of the *New Yorker*, Brian Moore's *The Colour of Blood* (1987), and David Lodge's *Nice Work* (1988). A reasonable cross-section of English writing, it would seem.

Such sentence adverbs do not necessarily stand at the beginning of sentences: 'The investigators, who must regretfully remain anonymous' (*Times Literary Supplement*, 1977); 'Aldabra Island in the Indian Ocean, where man "has thankfully failed to establish himself"' (*Times*, 1983).

Clearly, the question of the legitimacy of 'hopefully' as a sentence adverb branches out far beyond the domain of the actual word itself. The second edition of the *OED* has entries for *hopefully, regretfully, sadly, thankfully*, and perhaps one or two others, used as sentence adverbs. It draws attention to their unpopularity among 'some writers'. Most of the illustrative examples given in the dictionary to support the constructions are drawn from works written since the late 1960s.

What the twentieth-century evidence given in these entries fails to bring out is that the present widespread use of sentence adverbs is no more than an acceleration of a much older process. The *OED* entry for *seriously* (sense 1) has an example of 1644 drawn from the diary of Richard Symonds, who marched with the royal army during the Civil War: 'Except here and there an officer (and seriously I saw not above three or four that looked like a gentleman).' It is clear that 'seriously' does not directly qualify 'I' or 'saw' or 'gentleman', but the whole of the sentence that follows it. In 1872 Ruskin, in *The Eagle's Nest*, used the same adverb in the same manner: 'Quite seriously, all the vital functions . . . rise and set with the sun.' In both examples, 'seriously' is an elliptical use of the phrase 'to speak seriously'. The *OED* also cites a 1680 example of 'strictly' from the work of the printer Joseph Moxon, qualifying (as it says) 'a predication or assertion as a whole' (= strictly speaking); 'This whole Member is called the Moving Collar, though the Collar strictly is only the round Hole at *a*.' Other pre-twentieth-century adverbs used to qualify a sentence are not difficult to find: e.g. 'Frankly, if you can like my niece, win her' (Lord Lytton, 1847).

The proposition, then, can be amended to read as follows: since at least the seventeenth century, certain adverbs in *-ly* have acquired the ability to qualify a predication or assertion as a whole. Such adverbs are all elliptical uses of somewhat longer phrases. In the last third of the twentieth century, this little-used and scarcely observed mechanism of the language has broken loose. Any number of adverbs in *-ly* have come into common use as sentence adverbs. Conservative speakers, taken unawares by the sudden expansion of an unrecognized type of construction, have exploded with resentment, and with a level of resentment that is unlikely to fade away before at least the end of the century.

Sunday Times 1 October 1989

Suffixes: added to proper names

Aesopian, Betjemanesque, Borrovian, Heideggerian, Wittgen-steinian: such words crop up all the time in academic and general writing. Thus, from a recent encomium of the late Mark Boxer in the *London Review of Books*: 'his best efforts took him from . . . an aesthete's and illustrator's art to an account—more Proustian, or Powellian, than Swiftian—of the morals and manners of the Swinging London that ever was and isn't any more'.

The word *Aristotelian* apart, it was probably not until they reached the letter *B* that the editors of the *OED* began to face up to the problems presented by this kind of word. A policy of sorts began to emerge: in normal circumstances adjectives of this kind were not to be admitted to the *OED* until they were accompanied by a cluster of closely related forms. So *Baconian* and *Baconic* qualified because of the existence as well of *Baconianism* and *Baconist*; *Boswellian* because of *Boswellism* and *Boswellize*; and *Byronian* and *Byronic* because of *Byroniad, Byronist, Byronite,* and *Byronically*.

Throughout the *OED* the same policy of guarded admission was adhered to. Fame by itself was not enough, unless formations in *-iana, -ism, -ite, -ize,* and so on, were also found to exist. The editors were faced with infinite sets of adjectival formations if any adjectives formed on proper names were to be included. The nature of the inclusion/exclusion problem is neatly expressed in the *OED* entry for *-esque*: 'suffix, forming adjectives, represents French *-esque,* adapted from Italian *-esco* . . . In Italian derivatives in *-esco* are formed *ad libitum* on names of artists, and French and English writers on art have imitated this practice. Examples of such formations, not calling for separate notice in the Dictionary, are *Bramantesque, Claudesque, Turneresque.*'

In the *Supplement to the OED* (four volumes, 1972–86) my colleagues and I, somewhat grudgingly, made good some of the omissions. For example, to take only writers, entries were made for *Aeschylean, Alfredian, Anselmian, Anselmic, Arnoldian, Austen-ian,* and a few others in the letter *A*. The letter *B* contained entries for a few more such words—*Blakeian* (or *-ean, -ian*), *Borrovian, Brontëan, Brontesque, Browingesque, Burnsian,* and some other adjectives formed on the names of pre-twentieth-century writers, always with a small squad of related formations (*Browningese, Browningite, Burnsiana, Burnsite,* and so on). And so the pattern continued.

This somewhat *ad hoc* policy was forced on us by the circumstances of the time. The (mostly conservative) readers of sources copied examples of such words with the greatest reluctance even when requested to do so. Concordances were few and far between. Optical character reading lay in the future, as did the assembling of huge electronic databases of the types that now exist.

The meaning was normally expressed in a formulaic way: 'resembling the style of, partaking of the characteristics of', and the like. Such definitions, being easy to write, are like sweet spring water to lexicographers. Admittedly the *OED* had defined *Johnson-ian* a little more specifically: 'applied especially to a style of English abounding in words derived or made up from Latin, such as that of Dr Johnson'. But such particularity was very rare. Those who consulted the *OED* were expected to *know* what the chief attributes of the writers were, or else to seek them in other reference works.

This habit of appending *-esque*, *-(i)an*, or *-ic* (or, of course, *-ish* or *-like*) to the names of authors to indicate resemblance appears not to have begun until the sixteenth century (*Virgilian* is first recorded in 1513, *Platonic* in 1533), and then only rarely. The names of a few well-known classical writers are first recorded in adjectival form in seventeenth-century sources: *Aristotelian* in 1607, *Ovidian* 1617, *Pindaric* 1640, *Plinian* 1649, *Ciceronian* 1661, and *Ptolemaic* 1674. Of English names, *Drydenian* is even recorded during his own lifetime (1687). In the eighteenth century it was not unusual for such formations to be used very soon after the death of the writer concerned—thus *Gibbonian* 1794, *Johnsonian* (by Boswell) 1791, *Richardsonian* 1786—but, unless our records are faulty, most formations of this kind are not found until much later: *Fieldingesque* 1931, *Ouidaesque* ('marked by extravagance or lack of restraint') 1909. *Shakespearian* is not recorded before 1755.

The choice of suffix seems to have been mostly governed by euphony, but names that end in *-aw* or *-ow* normally have the latinate terminations *-avian* (*Shavian*) and *-ovian* (*Borrovian*) given to them. Some classical names have generated a cluster of adjectival forms since the seventeenth century—for example *Ptolemy*—but one of them (in this case *Ptolemaic*) usually settles down as the customary form.

There is one oddity. An unaccented final syllable of a name is normally lengthened and stressed when the adjectival form is made: thus *Alfred* but *Alfredian* (pronounced '-eed-' and bearing the main stress), and *Dryden* but *Drydenian* ('-een-'). For reasons of euphony, a good many names—Amis, Beddoes, Burgess, Byatt, for example—probably have to get by with fewer possible adjectival appendages than the likes of Byron.

Sunday Times 2 October 1988

Suffixes: nouns in *-ess*

'It is a serious inconvenience that neither *doctress* nor *doctoress* (*-tress* would be better) has been brought into any but facetious use as a prefixed title: the device of inserting a Christian name after *Doctor* (*Dr Mary Jones*) is clumsy, and sometimes (*Dr Evelyn Jones*) ineffectual.' So H. W. Fowler in *Modern English Usage* in 1926. Elsewhere in the book he provided three lists: established feminine titles (*abbess, duchess, princess*, etc.); recent or impugned ones (*authoress, manageress, poetess*, etc.); and words 'unfortunately' not provided with feminines (*councillor, president, teacher*, etc.). Now, nearly seventy years on, the case needs re-examining.

It should be borne in mind that *-ess* is a suffix of foreign origin. In so far as the Anglo-Saxons felt the need for a distinctive feminine suffix they favoured *-estre* (e.g. *lærestre*, female teacher; *hoppestre*, female dancer); as a specifically female ending it survives only (in a slightly disguised form) in *spinster*.

Immediately after the Conquest the first wave of words in *-ess* came into English from French (the suffix was ultimately of classical origin): *countess, duchess, empress, mistress, princess*, and many more. It was quickly seen to be a useful formative element in English and became attached to many established English words from the fourteenth century onwards, e.g. *Jewess* (fourteenth century, Wyclif), *patroness* (fifteenth century), *poetess* (sixteenth century, Tyndale), and so on.

These new words were formed either by substitution of *-ess* for *-er* (*adulterer/adulteress, murderer/murderess*, etc.) or by the addition of *-ess* to the stem of a common-gender word (*author/ authoress, giant/giantess*, etc.). When *-ess* was added to a noun ending in *-ter* or *-tor*, the vowel before the *r* was usually elided, e.g. *actress* (not *actoress*), *protectress, waitress*.

From the Middle English period until about 1850 the suffix retained its power as a more or less unrestricted means of indicating the femininity of an agent-noun. More than a hundred words in *-ess* denoting female persons or animals are listed in the *OED*. They vary greatly in currency and durability. Except for *lioness* (first recorded in the fourteenth century), *tigress* (1611), and to a more limited extent *leopardess* (1567) and *pantheress* (1862), the suffix is not used in any routine way of female animals. In *rectoress* (1729) and *vicaress* (1770), both now obsolete, the suffix means 'wife of a —'. Both words have other meanings as well. One of the senses of *mayoress* and of *ambassadress* is also 'wife of a —'. From about 1100 until about the middle of the nineteenth century a great many short-lived or facetious words in *-ess* slipped into the language: e.g. *confectioness* (only 1640), *entertainess* (only 1709), *farmeress* (1672–), *preacheress* (1649–), *saviouress* (1533–), and so on. They adorned the writings of Akenside, Latimer, Jeremy Taylor, and others. But for the most part they were used merely for contextual distinction or emphasis.

In the twentieth century three main types of words in *-ess* have been brought into question. First, *Jewess* and *Negress* have joined the list of words that are proscribed unless one happens to be Jewish or black oneself. The point is brought out, for example, in John Updike's *Beck: A Book* (1970): ' "In *Travel Light*, for example, you keep calling Roxanne a Negress." "But she was one." . . . "The fact is, the word has distinctly racist overtones." ' Updike, as narrator, comments 'it is as if there were holes in language, things that could not be named'.

Secondly, with varying degrees of stridency, ill-defined groups of people do not favour the use of distinctively feminine artistic terms such as *actress*, *authoress*, *poetess*, and *sculptress*, even though each of these words has a long (I almost said distinguished) history. It is argued that there is no need for such gender-marked terms, and that such words ought to go into the word-museum in which similar terms—e.g. *interpretress*, *philosopheress*, and *tutoress* —that once flourished, now find themselves.

Thirdly, several occupational terms in *-ess* are in retreat: e.g. *air hostess*, *shepherdess*, *stewardess*, and *waitress*. *Air hostess* and *stewardess* are gradually being replaced on English-language airlines by *flight attendant*; *shepherdess* has disappeared from farms and survives mainly in works of literary criticism; *waitress* is beginning to be threatened by two words from the awkward squad, *waitron* and *waitperson*.

Where will it all end? A thin curtain of social relegation is being wrapped round the word *manageress*. A woman priest is not called a *priestess*: *priestesses* belong to non-Christian religions. It looks as if the hard core of words in *-ess* that still survive—*ancestress, benefactress, governess, heiress, ogress, prophetess, seductress, temptress, votaress,* as well as *countess, duchess,* and so on—will remain in the language for a while. But for how long nobody can say.

Sunday Times 7 April 1991

Suffixes: verbs in *-en* formed from adjectives

In 1926 H. W. Fowler ventured to suggest that 'the average writer', if asked for an offhand opinion, would probably say that any adjective of one syllable had the power to produce a parallel verb ending in *-en*; thus *black* and *blacken*, *sad* and *sadden*, and so on. He then went on to show that the language did not work like that. We have, for example, *moist* and *moisten* but no *wetten* to answer to *wet*. This is not the place to give a full account of all such actual or notional pairs, but an examination of the evidence reveals some interesting tendencies.

First, there is no doubt that there is a substantial number (perhaps of the order of fifty) of standard verbs ending in *-en* that have been formed from adjectives. They include *blacken, brighten, broaden, cheapen, coarsen, dampen, darken, deaden, deafen, deepen, fatten, flatten, freshen, gladden, harden, lessen, lighten, liken, loosen, madden, moisten, quicken, quieten, redden, ripen, roughen, sadden, sharpen, shorten, sicken, slacken, smarten, soften, stiffen, straighten, sweeten, tauten, thicken, tighten, toughen, weaken, whiten, widen,* and *worsen.*

Examine the history of such pairs and it emerges that the process was at its most productive between 1200 and 1700. There is only one possible pair before the Conquest—the antecendents of *fast* and *fasten*—but the relationship of the two words is not at all straightforward. Sixteen of the words (*blacken, brighten, darken,* etc.) are first recorded from the Middle English period, that is effectively between 1200 and the late fifteenth century. They turn up in official papers, in private letters, and in theological tracts and poems. Just over twenty more of them (*cheapen, dampen, deaden,* etc.) entered the language in the sixteenth and seventeenth centuries. *Flatten* is first recorded in a poem by John Donne and *shorten* in Thomas More's *Richard III*.

By 1700 the formative power of the suffix had largely disappeared. The eighteenth century seems to have yielded only *broaden*, *madden*, and *tighten*. Dr Johnson illustrated his entry for the verb *broaden* with an example from Thomson's *Seasons*: 'Low walks the sun, and broadens by degrees, Just o'er the verge of day', with the comment 'I know not whether the word occurs, but in the following passage'. The *OED* showed that it did but could not find examples before Thomson. *Madden* is first found in a work (1735) by Alexander Pope, and *tighten* in one of Nathan Bailey's dictionaries (1727).

Interest quickened in such formations in the bookish world of the nineteenth century, but the dozen or so words of this type that are entered in the *OED* are nearly all marked 'rare' or else plainly were brought into existence to serve the metrical or other special needs of Victorian writers: e.g. 'Eyes, large always, slowly largen' (Coventry Patmore, 1844); 'When the child of God suffers his thoughts to wander, his affections to colden (A. B. Grosart, 1863).

To the best of my knowledge the suffix is no longer a living one. I have no record of any *-en* verb formed in the twentieth century from a one-syllabled adjective. The most recent one in my files is *neaten*, which is first recorded in 1898. Technically adjectives like *fab* (first recorded in 1961) and *naff* (1959) could produce *fabben* and *naffen* as verbs, but it seems unlikely that they will.

So far I have presented the case as if it is a simple matter of one-syllabled adjectives like *dead* yielding the verb *deaden*. But of course things are never as simple as that. Other patterns fall into several classes: (pairs in which the same form is used for both adjective and verb) *blind*, *foul*, *lame*, *still*, *wet*; (adjectives which have no corresponding verb in *-en* and no longer function as verbs themselves) *cold*, *good*, *grand*, *sore*; (a prefix added to form a verb rather than the suffix *-en*) *dense/condense*, *large/enlarge*, *new/renew*, *strange/estrange*; (no *-en* verb though the antonymic adjective has one) *cheapen* but not *dearen*, *deafen* but not *blinden*, *fatten* but not *thinnen* or *leanen*, *sweeten* but not *souren*.

There is another factor at work. Nearly all the *-en* verbs that first came into existence in the sixteenth and seventeenth centuries were preceded by words that were spelt the same as adjectives and verbs. Thus *deep* already existed as a verb in the Anglo-Saxon period; *deepen* did not join it and compete with it until the seventeenth century. *Moist* as a verb was used by Wyclif and Langland in the fourteenth century before being joined by *moisten* in the sixteenth century. All these battles went on a long time ago. The victorious forms have emerged. Only the remnants of the old conflicts between *-en* verbs and their unextended forms remain, and this kind of conflict is not bothering anyone in the twentieth century.

Sunday Times 10 March 1991

Unattached participles

Some grammarians call them dangling, hanging, or misrelated participles. H. W. Fowler called them unattached participles, and cited an example from a letter. 'Dear Sir, We beg to enclose herewith statement of your account for goods supplied, and *being desirous* of clearing our Books to end May will *you* kindly favour us with cheque in settlement per return, and much oblige.' The reply ran, 'Sirs, You have been misinformed. I have no wish to clear your books.' The mistake in the first letter was to attribute the desire to the wrong person.

Such failures to look ahead and consider the grammatical compatibility of the following clause are exceedingly common, especially in unscripted speech. Lord Belstead, speaking on Radio 4 in January about his own role after the resignation of Lord Whitelaw as Leader of the House of Lords, said: 'Being unique, I am not going in any way to imitate him.' He did not intend to imply that he was himself 'unique'. A commentator on *World at One* (BBC Radio 4) at the end of May spoke of the Reagan/Gorbachev summit: 'After inspecting a guard of honour, President Reagan's motorcade moved into the centre of Moscow.' Last December, Richard Ingrams wrote about the house in which he grew up: 'Now demolished, I can call it to mind in almost perfect detail.' Obviously the entire motorcade did not inspect the Russian troops, and Mr Ingrams had not been demolished.

Naturally such misrelated clauses are not restricted to unscripted speech: 'As one of our members paying by annual direct debit, we are sending you our 1987 handbook' (leaflet of the Professional Association of Teachers, 1987). 'Though originally attached to David, it is Gerry who will wait for her' (Channel 4 announcement about the television film *Echoes* by Maeve Binchy).

Fowler went on to approve of sentences in which certain participles have acquired the character of prepositions or adverbial phrases, and can stand before a noun or a clause without disturbing the logicality or grammatical soundness of the sentence: '*Talking of* test matches, who won the last?'; '*Considering* the circumstances, you were justified'; '*Roughly speaking*, they are identical'; '*Allowing for* exceptions, the rule may stand'. His judgement was surely right. In such examples the participial form is now normally seen to be in harmony with what follows. Modern examples come easily to hand: '*Assuming* her memory isn't impaired, she's aware of the mix-up, and if she chooses to ignore it, so be it'; '*Knowing* my mother, this is her way of punishing us' (both from letters in the *Chicago Tribune*, 1987); '"*Speaking of* money," said Beryl, "do you mind my asking what you did with yours?"' (Alice Munro, 1987). Somewhat more debatable is the use in scientific work of '*using*' as a semi-unattached participle: '*Using* carbon monoxide, his hiccups were cured for 30 minutes, but they came back again' (the writer, not his patient's hiccups, used carbon monoxide).

Some of the other key words in constructions of this type are *barring, excepting, given, granted, judging by, owing to* (first recorded as a prepositional phrase in the work of Sir Walter Scott), *provided, providing, seeing*, and *supposing*. Some of them can also be used with 'that', with an added touch of slight formality: 'Even *assuming that* the Socialist government was seriously committed . . . all this could only be accomplished . . .' (a 1986 issue of a sociological journal).

Many of the constructions are traced back to earlier centuries by the *OED*. For example, *considering* construed as a preposition with a simple object is found as early as the fourteenth century: 'And gentilly I preise wel thy wit, . . . *considerynge* thy yowthe' (Chaucer). *Provided (that)* and *providing (that)* construed as quasi-conjunctions have also been used for several centuries.

Modern examples of the various key words of this type are strewn about in books, journals, and newspapers in every part of the English-speaking world: '*Considering* his gene pool, Sean Thomas Harmon is probably among the better-looking babies born Monday' (*Chicago Tribune*, 1988); '*Given* bad light, . . . a nervous enemy firing this way and that may do most of our work for us' (Maurice Shadbolt, 1986, New Zealand); '*Granted*, it was not hard to interest a security man, who apart from a regular soldier had the most boring job on earth' (Thomas Keneally, 1985, Australia).

Unattached participles seldom lead to ambiguity. They just jar. But all those prepositional and conjunctional uses—*considering (that)*, *given (that)*, and so on—standing there quietly on the sideline, make the game of grammatical relatedness just that little bit harder to play.

Sunday Times 24 July 1988

Unstable cases

Before the Norman Conquest, English had a case-system not unlike that of Latin or Greek. Nouns fell into distinguishable groups to which were assigned the terms masculine, feminine, and neuter. They were also either 'strong' or 'weak'. The words that modified nouns—the definite article, adjectives, and so on—needed to be adjusted according to the company they kept. Anyone who has read English at Oxford will remember the torture imposed on them by the wondrous world of paradigms to the parts of which m., f., n., acc., g., d., sing., pl., etc., needed to be affixed.

The inflectional system, by internal readjustments or under the influence of the incoming Danes and Normans, or both, simplified itself. Distinctive dual forms (one for two people, another for more than two) of the first and second person plural pronouns disappeared. Nouns became invariable except in the possessive and when used as plurals. Adjectives and the definite article became invariable. Only the pronouns were left to carry the main weight of a greatly reduced case-system, but even this narrowed-down system is somewhat unstable.

Consider the reasonable view that elements before and after the verb *to be* should be in the same case. It works, of course, for nouns ('Paris is the capital of France'). It is no longer a safe rule for personal pronouns. In constructions introduced by *It is* or by *This* (or *That*) *is*, objective forms stream like refugees through the old barriers. Some stay, some migrate. *It's me* has for long been the natural form, not *It's I*. The older rigidities are maintained, however, if the pronoun happens to be qualified by a *who*-clause. There are also other constraints and assumptions as will be seen from the following examples from standard sources: (subjective) 'This time it was I who took the initiative' (Richard Cobb, 1985); 'It is we who are inappropriate. The painting was here first' (Penelope Lively, 1987); (objective) 'Too much of a·bloody infidel, that's me'

(Thomas Keneally, 1980); '"So . . ." says Jasper. "That's him, the old fraud."' (Penelope Lively, 1987); 'Can this be me? Driving a car?' (*New Yorker*, 1988).

After *as* and *than* there is considerable instability, depending on whether they are felt to be prepositions or conjunctions. The examples underline the fragility of any set rules: (subjective) 'I sensed that he was as apprehensive as I about our meeting' (Janet Frame, 1985); 'On the whole the men . . . are more formal and authoritarian in tone than she' (Marilyn Butler, 1987); 'the author . . . probably knows better than I what to say' (Tessa Strickland, 1990); (objective) 'I wanted you to be wiser than me, better than me' (Mewa Ramgobin, South African, 1986); 'The 1,700 paintings in the Uffizi have been described . . . by better qualified writers than me' (Peter Hillmore, 1987).

After *not*, except in informal speech ('Who banged that door?' 'Not me!'), the subjective forms of pronouns seem to be slightly in the ascendancy, but variation does occur: 'it must be he who's made of india-rubber, not I' (Angela Carter, 1984); 'it's you who are to blame, not me' (Mordecai Richler, 1980).

Apart from the notorious types 'Between you and I' and 'They asked John and I to do the job', there are numerous examples of pronominal case-switching that go more or less unnoticed in the informal circumstances in which they occur. They are all one-way journeys, that is objective forms are used where subjective forms would strictly be expected, not the other way round. The objective forms highlight the subject of the sentence in each case. Examples: (sentences led by *Me, I*) 'Me, I don't trust cats' (Garrison Keillor, 1989); 'Me, I'm thick-skinned, charming, vain and happy' (Robert Elms, 1989); (*me* + present participle) 'Me thinking I'd probably get some filthy fever in spite of the jabs' (Julian Barnes, 1989); (illogical, but bestowing emphasis on *me*) 'we sat down on either side of the radiogram, she with her tea, me with a pad and pencil' (Jeanette Winterson, 1985); (*Me too* as a reply to another person's assertion) '"Let's talk about each other, that's all I am interested in at the moment." "Me too," says Tom' (Penelope Lively, 1987); (in reply to a question) '"What do you make of that, Tonio?" "Me?" he said' (Brian Moore, 1987); (*me neither*) '"Too bad I can't reach the curtain." "Me neither," he said' (*New Yorker*, 1987); (*silly me*) '"After Diana had told me what Irena was asking?" "Of course. Silly me."' (Anthony Lejeune, 1986).

Case-loss is one of the most significant factors in the history of the language, the lingustic equivalent of a major earthquake. Relatively minor after-tremors, mainly brought about by a desire to give more prominence to the subject of a sentence, have occurred at intervals since the Conquest. More disturbances can be expected in the future.

Sunday Times 5 August 1990

Valentine messages

As everyone knows, St Valentine's Day, 14 February, has been marked since the Middle Ages by the choosing of sweethearts or the mating of birds. Chaucer mentions it in his *Parlement of Foules* (written about 1380), 'For this was on seynt Volantyns day Whan euery bryd comyth to chese his make [choose his mate]'. When the posting of personal letters and cards became popular, Valentine messages, at first formal ('a card of dainty design with verses or other words, especially of an amorous or sentimental nature, sent on St Valentine's day to a person of the opposite sex', *OED*), soon became commonplace. The *OED* cites a writer called Edward Nares who said in 1822 that 'the number of letters sent on Valentine's Day makes several additional sorters necessary at the Post Office in London'.

Leaving aside slightly concealed obscenities, what did we have this year in the columns and columns of messages printed in the national press? The terms of endearment tended as usual to be childlike combinations of recurring elements: *-pie* (*cutiepie, Dollypie, Honey Pie, Possum Pie, Sweetie Pie*); *-Poo(h)* (*Baby Pooh, Dec-Poos, ooh pooh, Poos, Smelly Pooh*); *-bum* (*cuddlebum, Honeybum Hound, Scrummybum, snugglebum*); *hot-* (*Hotlegs, Hotlips*); *-bun(s)* (*Cuddlebuns, Honeybun*); *-kin(s)* (*Babykins, Bearkin*); and fanciful animal names (*Angel Possum, Chuggypig, Honeybear, Pandapants, Pusspot, Snugglebee, Whiffterbee, Wrigglepuss*). Presumably the influence of Dame Edna Everage accounted for the possums.

Messages about permanence ('I love you now and forever', 'I will love you until the Sahara Desert freezes over') and inseparability ('Cheddar and Cheese have nothing on us') were ubiquitous. Some of the messages were totally obscure and seemed not to be addressed to a particular person: 'Awaiting an exposition of strawberries and mushrooms.' There was reference to Tom Sharpe's 'eighth novel' that seemed too clever by half.

A fair number of the messages were in Welsh, Spanish, French ('Je t'adore'), German, or Latin ('amor vincit omnia'), but these lacked inventiveness. It was enough, it seemed, to translate the fateful message into standard words in the target language.

The frequent misspellings of the lovelorn were allowed to stand: *queen of my skys, you make all my stiches hurt, truely, gorgeus, has'nt, did'nt, do'nt*, and so on. *Love* became *lerv* or *luv* often enough, and *you* turned up several times as *ya*.

There were hosts of invented words, most of them vaguely or overtly sexual: verbs like *chomple, rampatamp*, and *zoggle*, nouns like *bof* and *weeze*, and the adjective *rinky* ('have a rinky time'). *Ratbag, scumbag*, and *skunkworks* were used as purposeful terms of affection.

Physical characteristics were referred to again and again: *Big Ears, Big Nose, Floppy Ears*. The loved ones were often addressed as plants or animals: *Badger, Big/Little Bunny, Dormouse, Fox, Hedgehog, little bear, my little pickled onion, Piglet, Pomegranate, pussycat, Redbreast, Squirrel, Stringbean*, and *Sweet Pea*. Oddly, perhaps, obesity seemed not to be an obstacle to affection, to judge from *Fatsy, Fatty, Fatbelly Gutbucket*, and *Fattyberger*.

There was much disagreement about capitalization of all classes of words, but on the whole the addressed one was felt to deserve a capital initial. *Piglet* was deemed to be more affectionate than *piglet*. Again, the copy-editors did not intervene.

The bottom drawer of ingenuity was scoured for amorous-sounding nonsense words: *Angeldrawers, Boofuls, chickerbiddie, Cuddly Sniggle, Diddlie Wumps, higgle huggle, lion pixie nin, Poop-si-woop-si-woo, Sexorexic Fish, Snugglebuggly*, and *Wookey Pookie*. Reduplication was common: 'Panny Wanny Fanny From Issy Bissy Wissy Chrissy', 'Darling Nickywicky', 'Grottie Smottie Bundles of Kisses'. There were the usual lovers offering 'many smoochies' and declaring that 'we lovums you lotsums'. I didn't spot 'diddums' but doubtless it was there somewhere.

How is all this richly soppy nonsense transmitted from generation to generation? Some of it obviously goes back to A. A. Milne, Beatrix Potter, and (for all I know) Enid Blyton and other entertainers of the young. But a lot of it belongs to the territory of sound symbolism that J. R. Firth called 'phonaesthesia'. This is the area of language where particular sequences of letters come to be linked in the mind with recognizable semantic associations. Reduplication (*dilly-dally*, etc.) and the use of diminutive or affectionate suffixes like *-ie* (*wifie*) or *-pie* (see above) fall into this category. Professor Michael Samuels in his *Linguistic Evolution* (1972) focuses on the initial sound *sl-*; 'The phonaestheme /sl-/ may be assigned the values "slippery" or "falling" in *slide, slip, slime, slush, sludge, slough, slither, slink, sleek, slop(py), slaver, slobber, slur, slant, slope, sledge,* and possibly *sling* and *sleet*; and it may also be assigned the closely related values "inactive", "degenerate" or "morally worthless" in *slow, sloth, sleep(y), slumber, slack, slouch, sloppy, slug, sluggard, slut, slattern, slovenly, slump, slapdash, slang, slick* and to some extent in *sly, slander, slur, slate* (verb), *slum.*'

The language of the Valentine messages, year by year, is at any rate partially 'phonaesthetic', apart, that is, from being affectionate, dotty, and richly soppy.

Sunday Times 6 March 1988

Viewings and visitations

Alice Thomas Ellis wrote a piece in the *Spectator* recently about the lack of 'any recent information on what practical, immediate steps to take when Grandpa has breathed his last'. From a programme she had heard on the wireless (her word) she formed the view that 'the Americans seem to be shyer of death than we are—and, I would have said, crazier—but I'm not sure'.

With the help of an American friend, I have been looking into one practical, immediate step that many Americans take: the choice of (to us) somewhat unfamiliar wording in the death notices columns of their newspapers. In particular I have examined the wording used for the ordinary person's equivalent of the statesman's 'lying-in-state'.

First, though, a brief historical note. From the fifteenth century onward (so the *OED* informs us) the word used was *wake*: the watching (especially by night) of relatives and friends beside the body of a dead person from death to burial, or during part of that time. 'Now chiefly Anglo-Irish', the *OED* says (this entry was drafted about 1921).

The first record of the phrase *to lie in state* (where 'in state' means, as the *OED* has it, 'with great pomp and solemnity, with splendid or honorific trappings or insignia') is an entry in the *London Gazette* in 1705: 'Her Majesty is to lie in State in Hanover'.

My American friend sought help from friends and relations in Chicago, New York, Boston, Milwaukee, and elsewhere, and sent me a great many death notices, obituaries, and the like.

In America, it seems, Grandpapa's body is taken after death to a place that is most commonly called a 'Funeral Home' (or a 'Home for Funerals'), where it is prepared for burial and placed in a coffin or casket (the words are interchangeable in many parts of America) chosen by the next of kin. Such places may also be called 'Memorial Homes', 'Mortuaries', or 'Chapels'. Most of them sound like business premises: Leonard Memorial Home Ltd, Pierce Brothers Daley & Bartel Mortuary, and so on. The death notices frequently say that the deceased is 'resting', 'lying at rest', or 'reposing' at the Funeral Home. One declared that 'Gramma and great-Gramma' was 'now an angel'. All the customary details are provided: date of death, abundant and touching details of relationships (beloved husband of . . . , adored uncle of . . . , devoted grandmother of . . ., doubly devoted husband of . . . , adorable brother-in-law of . . . , proud gramma of seven, great-gramma of ten; and so on); often the cause of death (stated explicitly or implied by such formulas as 'in lieu of flowers, contributions to the Lymphoma Foundation'); and the time, date, and place, of burial (usually in fact of 'interment', unfortunately misprinted in one notice as 'internment') or cremation.

Nothing unusual about any of this. Such announcements form part of the grim duty of next of kin everywhere.

There was one distinguishing feature, however: in the great majority of notices, times and dates are given when friends and relatives are invited to come and pay their respects to the deceased. It turned out that *lying in state* had been democratized in America. Anyone at all can lie in state, not just princes and potentates, but this seems to happen in a church rather than a Funeral Home ('The remains will lie in state at church from 9 a.m. until time of service at 9.30 a.m.'). The ancient word *wake* is exceedingly common, and wakes can take place in a Funeral Home ('A wake for Pompilio will be held from 3 p.m. to 9 p.m. today and Tuesday at Lawrence Funeral Home') or sometimes form part of a religious service ('Liturgical wake service Friday 7.30 p.m. at Divine Word Chapel').

Much more commonly, though, the terms used for the paying of last respects to the dead in the day or days between death and burial were *visitation, viewing,* and *visiting,* each of them first used in this sense in the present century: 'Visitation at Felician Sisters Provincial House Friday 10 a.m. to 7 p.m.'; 'Final viewing 5 p.m. Mon. Oct. 17 at the Rowland Home for Funerals'; 'Visiting Glascott Funeral Home Inc., Sat., Sun. and Mon. 2–5 and 7–9 p.m.'.

The same idea was often expressed in other ways: 'Friends may call at the funeral home from 2 to 4 p.m.'; 'Calling hours Sunday evening 7 to 9'; 'Friends wil be received at the Ahern Funeral Home on Tuesday from 3 to 9 p.m.'. Occasionally people are dissuaded from making such calls: 'No visitation'; 'No visiting hours'.

My American friend thought that *viewing* was the term favoured in New Jersey (where he was born), *visitation* in Chicago, and *wake* or *visitation* in Boston, but he realized that the distribution of the terms would require further research.

Are the Americans shyer of death, as Alice Thomas Ellis thought? Or, on the evidence provided by the death notices I have seen, are they just slightly more insistent than we are on the retention of one of the traditional strands of respect and of grief? It is forty years since the publication of Evelyn Waugh's *The Loved One* and twenty-five years since Jessica Mitford's *The American Way of Death*. It is still an identifiably different way from ours.

Sunday Times 15 January 1989

Word formation

The origin and formation of the great majority of English words can be determined with reasonable certainty. Some of them—the core vocabulary of the language—arrived with the first Anglo-Saxon settlers, words like *blue, hand, land,* and *win*. They are demonstrably native words with cognates in most of the related languages: cf. German *blau, Hand, Land, gewinnen,* for example. Other words have joined the language in a fairly well understood and orderly way from external sources: from Greek (*angel, devil*), Latin (*altar, master*), Old Norse (*law, skin*), (Old) French (*charity, measure*), Middle Dutch (*huckster, splice*), Italian (*fiasco, intermezzo*), and so on. Words that are ultimately of Greek, Latin, or Arabic origin often entered English indirectly: for example, *algebra* and *sirocco,* both ultimately of Arabic origin, came into English via Italian. The third major source of new words is internal, that is

formations arising within the language itself, especially compounds like *coastguard* and *riverside*.

It is easy enough to construct an English sentence in which all
the words except articles and prepositions are of external origin:
e.g. 'Invading armies impose exotic political systems on conquered
countries'. Or one in which every word is of native origin: e.g.
'Hardly any horse-drawn ploughs are found in English fields now'.

In practice most English sentences contain a mixture of native
and external elements. In one of Ariel's songs in *The Tempest*
('Come vnto these yellow sands, And then take hands: Curtsied
when you haue, and kyst, The wild waves whist') the foreign
element happens to be slight: *take* (Old Norse) and *curtsied*
(French). In this modern sentence, 'The slatted shutters that
flanked the windows would be repainted, and the balustrade by the
steps' (William Trevor, 1988), the proportion of imported words
happens to be high: *slatted*, *flanked*, *repainted*, *balustrade*, all of
French origin, *window* Scandinavian. In general terms, however,
until the beginning of the twentieth century, Lewis Carroll apart,
the main sources of innovation were sensible compounding of
existing elements, or importation from a range of foreign languages,
especially from European ones (including ancient Greek and Latin).

It is instructive to examine some of the ways in which the
language has been diversified and supplemented in the twentieth
century. 'I'm not sure why I was DQ'd. They said I flipped over
before I turned,' Kriegsmann (a back-stroke swimmer) said (*Chicago
Tribune*, 1990). *DQ'd* means 'disqualified'. 'Housed on MIT's
campus, the foundation provides "copylefts" that ensure programs'
(*Computerworld*, 1990). *Copyleft* is formed from *copyright*.

Caris Davis's novel *Stealth* (1989) runs riot with ingenious, and
also not very lovable, blends, *hispanic* (= hip + Hispanic), *kidult*
(= kid + adult), *manimal* (= man + animal), and *wargasmic* (= war
+ orgasmic) among them. From American sources I have noted
advids (= admissions videotapes, sent by applicants to colleges and
universities of their choice), *croissandwich* (= croissant + sand-
wich), and *millyenaire* (= a Japanese millionaire). In 1953 W. F.
Scherer identified a particular strain of human epithelial cells, and
called it *HeLa* from the initial two letters of the name of Henrietta
Lacks, the patient from whom the original tissue was taken.
Clearly blending is one of the major means of forming new words
at the present time.

Another ancient and respectable process of word formation is the one known technically as conversion, i.e. the employment of an existing word as a different part of speech. This is the process by which the verbs *chair* (first recorded in 1552), *experience* (1533), *service* (1893), and *telephone* (1877) came into existence. Recent examples include *audible* (he audibled his allegations), *grocery-shop* (they can grocery-shop from behind the wheel of their car), and *transition* (programs to help them transition into becoming productive adults). They will not be to everyone's taste.

The language is also awash with acronyms, many of them now well established and fitting comfortably into the language. Others have nothing but ingenuity to commend them, e.g. *rurp* (= realized ultimate reality piton) and *smon* (= subacute myelo-optico-neuro-pathy, a disease of the nervous system).

The shock of the new is much less apparent in some other areas of word formation, though why this should be so is not altogether clear. Who has not smiled with pleasure while *gobsmacked* has made its swift way from northern counties into general use? Who but the victims find *handbagging* disagreeable? And perhaps even hapless Salman Rushdie could raise a rueful smile at the word *skoob*, formed by back-slang from the word *books* in 1963: 'A skoob tower by John Latham—a construction of art books designed to be detonated,' reported the *Architectual Review* in 1966. A *skoob* is 'a pile of books assembled in order to be destroyed as a gesture against the proliferation and undue veneration of the printed word'. But where is John Latham's skoob tower now?

Sunday Times 1 April 1990

Word origins: first impressions

One of the more or less self-evident truths about words and meanings is that, except for the most recent acquisitions to the language, the length of time that they have stood in the language has little bearing on the choices that writers make. The vocabulary of the day is made up of undifferentiated layers of words and meanings, undifferentiated, that is, in respect of the date of their entry into the language. There is only one main qualification to this statement: it usually takes slightly more than a century for a word to reach such a state of maturity that it is not recognizably or instinctively felt to be a newcomer. Thus *audio fair, sound cassette*, and *TV* clearly belong to our own century—who could doubt it? But which of us, without the aid of the *OED*, could with certainty assign a date of first record to words like *languorous, manicure* (verb), *penguin,* and *squeamish?* Such words are just part of our natural heritage. (The dates of first record are in fact 1490, 1889, 1578, and 1450 respectively).

This elementary proposition was easily confirmed by an analysis of the first three hundred words (that is, approximately a page) in each of three recent novels, Julian Barnes's *A History of the World in 10½ Chapters,* John le Carré's *The Russia House,* and Tom Wolfe's *The Bonfire of the Vanities.*

First, I eliminated from consideration all the ordinary workaday words of the language—articles, prepositions, conjunctions, pronouns, numerals, the verbs *be, do,* and *have,* and the modal verbs *can, could, must,* etc. These essential pieces of language building and joinery accounted for 57 per cent of the text in Barnes, 44 per cent in le Carré, and 47 per cent in Wolfe.

Barnes yielded an almost equal number of words of native origin (*Ark, bird, bright, child,* etc.) and of French (or Latin) origin (*comfort, dangerous, decision, nursery,* etc.); so did le Carré (native: *asleep, broad, brown, cram,* etc; French or Latin: *appropriate, ceiling, council, culture,* etc.). By contrast, Wolfe's passage showed an overwhelming preference for words of native origin (*barely, cackle, crowd, heckler,* etc.), with only a few words of French or Latin origin showing up (*actual, bigot, fantastic, impudence,* etc.).

Words from every century since the Anglo-Saxon period down to the nineteenth century occurred in all three passages: (Barnes) *stench* OE, *large* 12th century, *comfort* 13th, *delicate* 14th, *fastidious* 15th, *nursery* 16th, *exist* 17th, *roulette* 18th, *messy* 19th; (le Carré) *old* OE, *council* 12th, *hideous* 13th, *appropriate* 14th, *blasphemous* 15th, *beach* 16th, *staircase* 17th, *feature* (verb) 18th, *deck chair* 19th; (Wolfe) *deep* OE, *somewhere* 12th, *air* 13th, *actual* 14th, *glare* (noun) 15th, *bigot* 16th, *erupt* 17th, *haze* 18th, *okay* 19th.

Except for *dental hygienist*, Barnes's passage lacks twentieth-century neologisms and leaves one with a cautious first impression of linguistic conservatism. The other two have no such inhibitions: (le Carré) *audio fair, betting shop, sound-booth, sound cassette;* (Wolfe) *black community, Charlie* (=white man), *down-home* (= homespun), *code name, go* (= say), *gonna* (going to), *racist, TV.*

They stand out like skyscrapers as linguistic beacons of our own age.

Curiously, there are expressions in all three passages, some of them contextually formed and ephemeral, others looking more permanent, that have not yet made their way into the largest dictionaries: (Barnes) *cleaner-bird, fire-tongue, winch-work*; (le Carré) *audio fair, computer English, sound-booth, sound cassette*; (Wolfe) *belly sound, black community*. The lexicographers' trawling nets are doubtless gathering them up.

What can be made of all this? The first impression one gains from an examination of these three short passages is that Julian Barnes is linguistically fastidious, very British (no transatlanticisms admitted), a writer who, beneath a slightly mocking veneer, keeps a tight rein on his choice of vocabulary and constructions. John le Carré's vocabulary in this passage is plain, matter-of-fact, un-garnished, but thoroughly up to date. He uses *launch* (as a noun) instead of *launching* of an exhibition that was being opened in Leningrad. He is not above the occasional cliché like 'its excruciating end'. The style is less important than the story. Wolfe stands a full ocean away. The words and rhythms of an aggressive group of American blacks are caught to perfection. 'Don't you shine us up with no more your figures!', they cry, meaning 'Don't try to flatter us with any more of your figures'. Words are run together (*gonna* = going to, *inna* = in the). There are outrageously convincing representations of the din of shouting voices: 'Hehheheh . . .unnnnhhhh-hunhh!'

Of course these are only the first impressions that the three writers give of their work, the point of entry to three absorbingly interesting works. But, as Martin Chuzzlewit remarked to Tom Pinch in Chapter 5 of Dickens's novel, 'First impressions, you know, often go a long way, and last a long time.' It's a trite enough view, but I think it truly applies to the first three hundred words of these three novels.

Sunday Times 20 August 1989

4

Individual Words and Constructions

ain't

'Do you hear? Don't say "ain't" or "dang" or "son of a buck" . . . You're not a pair of hicks!' scolds a mother to her children in a *New Yorker* short story. '"Fritz That's It" ain't' was the headline to a news item about the closing of a salad bar with the wonderful name of 'Fritz That's It'. 'Some people are poor, some are unhappy, some are rich and selfish, . . . there is famine and war—ain't it a rotten shame?' said Brian Walden in the *Sunday Times*.

Ain't is not much of a word to get excited about, one would have thought. But excitement and it are often directly related. In 1942 Eric Partridge remarked that using *ain't* for *isn't* is 'an error so illiterate that I blush to record it'. In 1961 *Webster's Third New International Dictionary* listed the word with only mild admonishment ('though disapproved by many and more common in less educated speech, used orally in most parts of the U.S. by many cultivated speakers esp. in the phrase *ain't I*'), and found itself virtually placed in the stocks for this entry alone. Dictionaries of current English tend to hold the word, as it were, in a pair of tweezers. The label 'colloquial' is applied to it. None admits it to the sacred unqualified ranks of Standard English.

Ain't is an undisputed element in Cockney speech, whether in Dickens ('You seem to have a good sister.' 'She ain't half bad.') or in the deliciously outrageous rantings of Alf Garnett. Trendy papers on popular music tend to associate the word with American blacks: a Rap singer called LLCoolJ (= Ladies Love Cool James) in a recent issue of the *International Musician* is reported as saying 'My music sounds kinda real to me—it ain't no fantasy'. The Australian lawyer Malcolm Turnbull (of *Spycatcher* fame), in an article on the Down Under bicentennial, said that 'The Queen . . . is an Englishwoman, the greatest this century. But an Aussie she ain't.'

How did the word come about? And why do some people use it

naturally, while others regard its use as a sign of irretrievable vulgarity?

Its spelling is odd. In constructions of the type *am, is, are, have* + *not*, the word *not* in unabbreviated form is written separately whether or not the first element is contracted: *am not/'m not, is not/'s not, are not/'re not, has not/'s not, have not/'ve not*. When the negative itself is contracted, it combines with the full form of the preceding element: *isn't, aren't, wasn't, weren't, hasn't, haven't* (not *'sn't, 'ren't*, etc.). The form *ain't* is the odd man out. It is not a reduced form of any logical ancestor. Properly speaking, the last element in a tag-question of the type 'I am here, am I not?', if reduced, should be *amn't I*, as it is in many modes of speech in Scotland and Ireland. But Standard English has opted instead for the totally illogical *aren't I*,[1] a stiffnecked Sassanach use if ever there was one from the point of view of the Scots.

So what are we dealing with here? The word *ain't* has been recorded in the popular speech of London and elsewhere since 1778. It has made its way into a host of catchphrases and songs: 'ain't it grand to be blooming well dead?'; 'ain't love grand?'; 'there ain't no such animal'; 'ain't that something?'; 'it ain't necessarily so'; 'if it ain't broke don't fix it'; 'Is you is or is you ain't my baby?'

It flourishes in Black Vernacular English in the United States, where it has also acquired the meanings 'do not, does not, did not' ('Ain't you know Felo ben stay'n wid me?'). It is used by many Americans, white as well as black, in a manner that they might

---

[1] *Comments from readers.* 'It has long seemed to me likely that the first element of *aren't I* is a south-of-England "mistaken" spelling of *an't = amn't*. Hearing *an't* (rhyming with *pant, rant* etc.) a southern speaker would be likely to make it conform in his pronunciation to the commoner southern vowel in *chant, plant* etc. on the powerful analogies of *can't* and *shan't*, which on this view would have made a similar change of vowel. The difference is that a southern speaker reading *can't* and *shan't* would be in no doubt how to pronounce them; he would be in difficulties with *an't*, which looks very like *ant* and in days gone by would often have been identical with it. *Aren't* would have suited him much better phonetically as both writer and reader. But I feel there must be objections to this hypothesis or you would have mentioned it in your article.' (Kingsley Amis, private letter of 11 July 1988)

'Dr Burchfield is wrong to brand *aren't I* as totally illogical. When followed by *n't*, *am* behaves exactly like *can* and *shall*, losing its final consonant and (in standard English) lengthening its vowel. The expected spelling would be *an't*, but in those forms of English which lose pre-consonantal *r* the short form of *am not* merges with that of *are not* in both speech and spelling. I suspect that the Scottish *amn't I?* is a posh substitute for the demotic "am I no?". (David McLintock in *Sunday Times* 17 July 1988)

describe as 'cute': 'Phylicia Ayers-Allen who plays Bill Cosby's wife on the Cosby TV show—is she or ain't she married in real life?' Alexander Haig recently said of George Bush: 'Anybody who has to spend all his time demonstrating his manhood has somehow got to know he ain't got it.'

Yale alumni presumably consider themselves 'cultivated speakers'. The *Yale Alumni Magazine* recently recorded one Wilbur Woodland as saying 'Still working the Cape Cod and Florida cycle. And it ain't too bad.'

Ain't is a necessary part of the vocabulary of comic strips. 'Hägar the Horrible', for example, shows a Viking-type warrior in bed and reluctant to get up. The ballooned words read 'It ain't a question of "when", but *can* I get up?!'

For over 200 years the bar sinister word *ain't* has been begging for admission to Standard English. In tag-questions it has been thwarted by the equally bar sinister form *aren't*. In other uses it leads a shadowy existence in the language of various underclasses. It stands, as it were, at the door, out on the pavement, not yet part of any standard paradigm in the drawing room, except of course in catchphrases and in other contexts of referential humour.

Sunday Times 10 July 1988

and

The simplest-looking words are often among the most complicated and *and* is no exception. The normal function of this connective conjunction is, of course, to join sentence elements of the same kind: e.g. *Dido and Aeneas; first and foremost; the compensations and inducements are generous; she served quickly and efficiently; for ever and ever; an acute and wary sense of the ordinary.* It can imply progression (*faster and faster*), causation (*Misbehave and you'll not get your pocket money*), great duration (*she ran and ran*), a large number or a great quantity (*miles and miles, piles and piles*), and addition (*four and four are eight*).

In practice *and* is often omitted for contextual effects of various kinds, especially when two or more adjectives occur in conjunction. Thus, from my files: (without *and* and using a comma or commas instead) 'Czechs were marginal, remote, troublesome, peculiar Europeans with unpronounceable names'; (without *and* and without commas) 'he envied Jenkin his simple uncluttered uncomplicated innocent life' (Iris Murdoch, 1987).

There is a persistent belief that it is improper to begin a sentence with *And*, but this prohibition has been cheerfully ignored by standard authors from Anglo-Saxon times onwards. An initial *And* is a useful aid to writers as the narrative continues. The *OED* provides examples from the ninth century to the nineteenth, including one from Shakespeare's *King John*: 'ARTHUR. Must you with hot Irons, burne out both mine eyes? HUBERT. Yong Boy, I must. ARTHUR. And will you? HUBERT. And I will.' It is also used for other rhetorical purposes, and sometimes just to introduce an improvised afterthought: 'Tibba still pined and slavered for the school lunches. And little other care hath she' (A. N. Wilson, 1982); '"I'm going to swim. And don't you dare watch"' (Gwendoline Butler, 1983); '"Altogether encircled?" "And nowhere to go," Blewitt confirmed' (Maurice Shadbolt, 1986). It is also used in expressing surprise at, or asking the truth of, what one has already heard: 'O John! and you have seen him! And are you really going?' (1884 in *OED*).

Another well-established use of *and* is in the phrase *and all*. Wright's *English Dialect Dictionary* gives prominence to this use, meaning 'and everything; also, besides, in addition'. In some of the examples it seems to lack any perceptible lexical sense and to be just a rhythmical device to eke out a sentence. Wright's nineteenth-century evidence is drawn from almost every county and he also lists examples from dialectal contexts in the works of Tennyson, Gissing, Kipling, and others: (Scottish) 'Woo'd and married an' a''; (Westmorland) 'When she saw me she wept; I wept ano''; (West Yorkshire) 'Whoy, we'n been up an darn anole'; (Lincolnshire) 'He wants sendin' to Ketton [Kirton-in-Lindsey prison], an a-cat-o'-nine-tails an'-all'. The use has seeped out into more general use in our own century: 'When I held her in my arms she was like a dying bird, so thin and all' (Michael Doane, 1988); 'We had a hell of a job pushing it, what with the sarnie-boards and all' (Caris Davis, 1989); 'Yes, he's remarried and all, and has more family' (Rick Rofihe, *New Yorker*, 1990).

A cricket commentator on BBC TV said wearily at the end of a barren over in the first test by the West Indian bowler Curtly Ambrose, 'There are maidens and there are maidens, but that wasn't one of the best.' He was using a construction first recorded in English in the sixteenth century 'expressing a difference of quality between things of the same name or class', as the *OED* expresses it. The use, the Dictionary says, is 'commonly called a French idiom' and refers to Molière's "il y a fagots et fagots" in *Le Médecin malgré lui* (1666), but the English evidence is earlier. The *OED* cites examples from the sixteenth to the nineteenth centuries, including 'Alack, there be roses and roses, John!' (Browning, 1855). To which may be added the following nineteenth- and twentieth-century examples: 'Well, as to that, of course there are kings and kings. When I say I detest kings, I mean I detest *bad* kings' (W. S. Gilbert, *The Gondoliers*, 1889); 'There are Coloureds and Coloureds, just as there are whites and whites' (Dalene Matthee, 1986); 'There were ways to steal and ways to steal' (*New Yorker*, 1988); (in a context of a weapon to use against a pit-bull terrier) 'It was even as I took this on board that it came to me that there were walking-sticks and there were walking-sticks. What I needed was a fortified whangee' (Alan Coren, 1991); 'There is homelessness and home-lessness. The word has become a shibboleth for opposition politicians and the "caring" media . . . The sort of homelessness which means despair is quite different from the sort which means adventure' (Janet Daley, feature article in *The Times*, 1991).

I told you there are *ands* and there are *ands*. And yet we hardly notice the word at all in either written or spoken English.

Sunday Times 14 July 1991

anyone . . . their

Until about thirty years ago it was normal enough to say 'anybody can see for himself', 'everyone was blowing his nose', or 'it's every man for himself', even when women were present. From Anglo-Saxon times onward, *his*, *him*, or *himself* were used, in a reasonably limited range of contexts, to refer to a person of either sex. If someone happened to ask 'May I see the doctor himself?' and the reply turned out to be 'Dr Mary Smith will see you at 10 a.m.', hackles were not raised. It was just the way the language worked. For some 1,200 years the language had opted for the masculine form of the pronouns when the context referred to persons of either sex. There was no problem, or so it seemed, until the feminists came into view.

In the 1950s strident voices rose up in wrath. Articles were written and new slogans were invented. *Ms* and *chairperson* (and then *chair*) were devised, as well as scores of other *-persons* (*craftsperson, salesperson,* etc.). The major airlines began to call their stewardesses *flight attendants.* Other neutral words like *photographer* (not *cameraman*) were insisted on. New editions of dictionaries tended to redefine *rape* as 'commit rape on (person)' instead of 'commit rape on (woman)'.

For a time, now mercifully in the past, attempts were made to manufacture a composite set of pronouns meaning 'he or she', 'him or her', 'his or her', and 'his or hers'. A Chicago superintendent of schools apparently proposed for this purpose the set 'he'er, him'er, his'er, and his'er's'. She tried to get the National Education Association to accept them, but without success. A comedian in *Forbes* magazine blended 'he, she, or it' to produce 'h'orsh'it'! The only composite forms to emerge and fall into quite customary use were 's/he' and 'him/herself', though these are written forms only with no comfortable spoken equivalents.

While the experimentation was going on, the obvious though somewhat cumbersome convention of doubling pronouns came roaring into fashion all over the English-speaking world: 'the artful doctor may find a moment in which to exercise his or her art' (USA, 1986); 'let the receiver choose exactly what he or she would like' (India, 1986); 'the concept embraces . . . buying space in his or her publication to promote your product' (South Africa, 1984); 'the teacher him/herself must be genuinely relaxed' (UK, 1987); 'the tragedy of a depressive's position is that he or she remains frozen in front of the mirror' (UK, 1987).

In broad terms then, with minor exceptions, the pronominal system has survived the feminist drive almost unscathed, though the more ardent feminists doubtless still dream about stumbling on a perfect genderless set of pronouns for use in contexts referring to persons of either sex.

For quite some time, though the use has a modern feel about it, a different method of avoiding the type 'he or she' has been resorted to. It began in the fifteenth century. The pronouns *they, them, their,* and *themselves* have been employed (as the *OED* expresses it) 'in reference to a singular noun made universal by *every, any, no,* etc., or applicable to one of either sex (= "he or she")'. Thus, 'Eche of theym sholde . . . make theymselfe redy' (Caxton, 1489); 'Euery one to rest themselves [ed. 1594 himselfe] betake' (Shakespeare, 1600); 'Every Body fell a laughing, as how could they help it' (Fielding, 1749); 'If a person is born of a gloomy temper . . . they cannot help it' (Chesterfield, 1759); 'Nobody else . . . has so little to plague them' (Charlotte Yonge, 1853); 'Now, nobody does anything well that they cannot help doing' (Ruskin, 1866). And, in particular, blatantly breaking strict rules of concord, 'a person can't help their birth' (Thackeray, 1848), and 'It's enough to drive anyone out of their senses' (G. B. Shaw, 1898). The *OED* does not condemn these uses in any way.

Old habits continue, and it is easy to find similar examples in the 1980s. Thus, from my files: 'Does anyone want their coffee black?'; 'an invaluable resource for everyone who wants to express themselves'; 'Someone could be running Mitchell as their stalking horse'; 'Why would anyone plan their own funeral?'; 'The heat was up so high that almost everyone took off their coats'; 'If a player throws a 6 and a 3 they have the option of moving 3, 6 or 9 spaces'. Even good writers find such constructions hard to avoid in informal contexts.

Less defensible is the use of the illogical form *themself*. It is not very common but it is beginning to appear in print. A 1986 circular of the Samaritans contains the sentence 'By the time you finish reading this letter someone will have tried to kill themself'. In such desperately sad circumstances one is tempted to let grammatical faults pass. But a fault it is nevertheless.

Sunday Times 29 May 1988

baggage

My wife and I were somewhere above the Atlantic when the voice of an American woman was heard saying, 'Is this the way to the bathroom?' She was not in a bathrobe, of course, and in any case there was no bathtub (as she would doubtless call it) to bathe (British 'to bath') or take a bath in. The British Airways flight attendant instantly translated before replying, 'No, madam, what you are looking for is at the rear of the compartment.' It was a trifling example of the way in which we have all become partially bilingual now. Of course other terms were available to the American passenger—*washroom, restroom, ladies' room, powder room*, and so on—but her choice happened to be *bathroom*. The air hostess equally, with all proper courtesy, could have used *loo, lavatory*, or (with a slight change of tone) *toilet* in her reply without any loss of intelligibility. All of us carry around a lockerful of synonyms for central concepts, and emerge mostly unpuzzled from casual requests made by overseas questioners.

Let me enlarge on this concept of partial bilingualism. To many standard speakers in Britain the word *baggage* in its primary sense has a residual American flavour (as Fowler asserted in *Modern English Usage*), perhaps as a legacy of the baggage trains and baggage wagons of the pioneering days in the American west. By contrast the customary or traditional word in Britain at one time was normally *luggage*. When I started to investigate the currency of the two terms my working assumption was that *baggage* was perhaps still as markedly American and *luggage* as markedly British as, say, *cookie* and *biscuit*. *Luggage* and *baggage* had been used alternately and synonymously by the uncouth Sir Pitt Crawley in Thackeray's *Vanity Fair*, but this was probably an isolated case.

I called in all the resources available to me: dictionaries, concordances, newspapers, computerized databases, and personal observation at airports and railway and road transport terminals. Meanwhile an American friend was prowling about on the same mission, especially in Illinois. I examined public signs at airports in Dallas, Auckland, Tahiti, and Gatwick, and at Paddington and other railway stations.

What was the result? It seems that, with the arrival of mass air travel, *baggage* and *luggage* have acquired dual, and then multiple, nationality as words. A story in the *Daily Telegraph* spoke of 'baggage supervisors at luggage carousels'. The *Washington Post* reported that 'passengers' luggage that came through the baggage claim area had been badly damaged'. The *Chicago Tribune* (23 December 1987) carried a headline 'Somewhere 10 baggage handlers are all wearing numbered jerseys', and the news item began, 'The Engineers of Rose-Hulman Institute of Terre Haute left for a playing tour of Europe and the Soviet Union earlier this month, but their luggage didn't.'

It is not quite a case of total interchangeability. A few phrases seem to be more or less fixed throughout the English-speaking world: thus *excess baggage* (not *excess luggage*), *baggage area* (but see below), *baggage claim*, *baggage handlers*, *baggage handling* are the norm. At air terminals *hand baggage* and *hand luggage* seem to be used with about equal frequency. In the United States a person who looks after the checked bags of passengers on a train is always a *baggageman*. The same word is used there for a baggage porter in a hotel. If you look at the relevant compartment in your local 125 train you will probably find the word *Luggage* used as a label on the shelves. There was still a *Luggage locker* sign at Paddington Station in February this year. Tradition will probably keep such signs intact. On the other hand Gatwick airport (April 1988) had a sign *Left baggage* in its main arrivals terminal.

In his *Cut-Rate Kingdom*, Thomas Keneally's Australian soldiers slept on the luggage rack. One of Bernice Rubens's characters in her novel *Our Father* 'busied herself with her luggage . . . Not that Veronica sported much baggage.' In A. L. Barker's *The Gooseboy*, though, 'The plane started bucking, and there was a noise from the luggage area as if a pride of lions was breaking out.' Ms Barker seems to know her luggage from her baggage.

None of this chopping and changing troubles any of us now. Brows are no longer wrinkled at the loss of this small traditional distinction. In figurative uses, however, the customary word everywhere seems to be *baggage* and *baggage* alone: 'some emotional baggage of my own' (*New Yorker*); 'a pragmatist who travels light, without cumbersome ideological baggage' (*Financial Times*).

Bathroom, loo, toilet, lavatory, baggage, luggage: such words are swirling round the English-speaking world. We pick our way among them, selecting this word or that to suit our taste. But we have a wide acceptance basket if someone from America, Australia, or anywhere else, uses one of the terms that we avoid using ourselves.

Sunday Times 1 May 1988

because

It's the fault of the French really. In the fourteenth century, English speakers began to place the ubiquitous native prefix *be-* (or *bi-* or *by-*) in front of the French word *cause* in a splendid array of conjunctional uses: 'By cause Nero hadde of hym swiche drede', 'Bycause that the cradel by it stood' (both from Chaucer); 'I moste seie forth my servise. Bi-cause whi hit is clerkes wyse' (*In a Chirche*, 1390). It was sometimes preceded and strengthened by *for*: 'For be-cause that I know the sorw [sorrow] that they have' (a fifteenth-century sermon). The meanings multiplied—'for the reason that', 'inasmuch as', 'since', 'in order that'—and the constructions thrived. The word *because*, often preceded or followed by governing elements like *for*, *that*, or *why*, took hold and became part of the normal furniture of standard English.

Anyone who has cycled through a course of Middle English and Tudor texts knows how to change gear slightly as the humps and bumps of such constructions turn up. The difficulties are easily overcome, including contexts where rival constructions like *for cause that* and *for cause of* are used instead of *by the cause that* and *by the cause of*.

As all this was happening, the word *reason* (from French) preceded by *bi* or *by* was steadily making its way into the same or very similar territory. And then, predictably but tautologically, the two constructions merged to admit 'the reason . . . was because' alongside the standard type 'the reason . . . was that'.

So how does *because* now stand, towards the end of the 1980s? Used as a conjunction it normally introduces a dependent clause expressing the cause, reason, or motive of the content of the main clause: 'she wept because she loved him' (the *because*-clause, here following the main clause, answers the question 'why?'); 'because we were running short of petrol, we began to look for a garage' (the *because*-clause precedes the main clause); 'I know he's at work, because his wife told me' (answering the question 'how do you know?'); 'she thinks I'm upset because I wanted Fred to spend the night' (answering the question 'why does she think that?'); (preceded by 'just') ' "And all they are doing is sitting around on their high-priced butts drinking tea, just because they haven't had your scripts." "My word," said Henry.' All these, including the last from Malcolm Bradbury's *Cuts* (1987), are well-regulated uses of *because*.

Also acceptable, in informal use, is the unadorned retort 'Because!', with the implication that a fuller reply is being withheld for some reason. ' "Why didn't you leave the bottle?" "Because!" I said shortly. I wasn't going to explain my feelings on the matter.'

More questionable *because*-clauses, in order of increasing un-acceptability, are: (1) 'I know he's at work because his car is not in the garage and his wife told me' (a mixture of two constructions). (2) 'He did not go to South Africa because he loved the game of rugby.' Examine it carefully for its ambiguity. It is often unsafe to place *because* after a clause containing a negative. (3) In con-structions with *why* and *because* placed in that order: 'he was implying that why he knew she had kept the promise was because he had been seeing Arnold'; 'why I spoke sharply was because she was rude'. Such constructions are sometimes called 'pseudo-cleft sentences'. (4) Though often defended by modern grammarians, the type 'the reason . . . is because' (instead of 'the reason . . . is that') aches with redundancy, and is still as inadmissible in standard English as it was when H. W. Fowler objected to it in 1926.

A sub-editor of *The Times* should not have allowed *because* to stand on the front page of the issue of 19 January this year: 'He [Dr David Owen] had believed the reason for Mr MacLennan's visit was because he had doubts about the new policy.' There was a great deal of muddlement and confusion that night without the introduction of grammatical redundancy as well. It is better to leave such constructions to the largely grammarless world of trendy magazines: 'One of the reasons . . . that singers like Randy Travis and Dwight Yoakam have sold themselves so successfully in this country is because they are selling authenticity' (*The Face*, 1987). Authenticity, for all I know, truly belongs to Randy and Dwight, but grammar, I suspect, is well down the list of priorities for their fans. The redundant construction is even occasionally found in much more elevated sources: (from a set of papers on the history of linguistics) 'The reason for the continued success of this physical atomism was because it was consistent in explaining a wide variety of new experimental results' (C. Gilman, 1987). We may see more of it in the future.

Sunday Times 17 April 1988

Note from a correspondent: 'Your very interesting survey of *because* omits two of the most remarkable uses of this item.

The first is the use of *because* to mean "and the proof is that", as illustrated by such examples as "It must be raining in the mountains because the river's full". Normally, in a sentence of the form "p because q", *q* is given as the cause of *p*, but in examples such as this one, the causal relationship, insofar as there is one, is the other way round. Interestingly, none of the dictionaries at my disposal recognizes this usage except for the Longman, which characterizes it as "inappropriate to formal use" and recommends that *because* be replaced by *for* in such cases.

The second, and more extraordinary, use of *because* is one which appears to be particularly beloved of television interviewers, as a result of which my colleague, Dr Roger Wright, has dubbed it the "BBC *because*". The striking thing about this use is that the *because* clause follows, not a statement, but a question, as in the following example: "Why has the Afghan government agreed to the Soviet withdrawal, because the fighting is sure to go on?" This particular example is less bizarre than some, but note the following genuine example: "Are you competing in Oslo, because you're not, surely?"

In both these uses, the occurrence of *because* appears to be explicable only by the postulation of some sort of ellipsis. In the first type, "p because q" can, not too implausibly, be interpreted as an ellipsis of "(I infer p) because q". The second type is more troublesome, but there appears to be the basis of an account along the lines of "(I'm asking you about p) because q".' (Dr R. L. Trask, private letter of 18 April 1988)

between

The nation is divided in its use of 'between you and me' and 'between you and I'. Let me begin by declaring that the only admissible construction of the two in standard use in the twentieth century is 'between you and me'. I know that Bassanio read out a letter to Portia containing the sentence 'All debts are cleerd betweene you and I if I might but see you at my death', and that Mistress Page said that 'there is such a league betweene my goodman, and he'. So be it. Goneril, on the other hand, said 'There is further complement of leaue-taking betweene France and *him*' (not *he*). *I*, *he*, and other pronouns were frequently used in the sixteenth and seventeenth centuries in ways now regarded as ungrammatical. Grammatical assumptions were different then, especially when the pronoun in question was separated from the governing word by other words.

The boundaries are much less clearly drawn in the use of *between* and *among*. Many people cling to the idea that *between* is used of two and *among* of many, but the *OED* maintains that 'In all senses, *between* has been, from its earliest appearance, extended to more than two . . . It is still the only word available to express the relation of a thing to many surrounding things severally and individually, *among* expressing a relation to them collectively and vaguely.' The *OED* further divides the uses of *between* into four main branches: of simple position; of intervening space; of relation to things acting conjointly or participating in action; of separation. These distinctions are needed to account for the wide fluctuations of usage over the last eight centuries.

The main present-day patterns can be fairly clearly discerned, I think, in the following examples: (two persons or things) 'Things that had happened a long time since—between Isaac and myself'

(Nigel Williams, 1985); 'Museums have become an uneasy cross between theatre and boutique' (*New Yorker*, 1987); (more than two persons or things) 'Dividing his time between engineering, mechanical inventions, and writing for periodicals' (G. S. Haight, 1968); 'The death of his sister had changed things between Marcus, Ruth and Jacqueline' (A. S. Byatt, 1985); 'For Sale and Rent . . . Situated between Florence, Siena, Perugia. Easy Access Rome' (*London Review of Books*, 1986); (number of events, groups, etc., less clearly defined) 'Does he sigh between the chimes of the clock?' (J. M. Coetzee, 1977); (borderline cases where *among* should perhaps have been used) 'I want to walk between the trees and smell them too' (Elizabeth Jolley, 1980); 'A company has £25 million of profit to distribute between 10,000 workers' (*The Times*, 1987).

Contrast *among* 'expressing a relation to many surrounding things collectively and vaguely', as the *OED* has it: 'There's only us . . . left among the wreckage' (Stan Barstow, 1960); 'There were a lot of very young people among the temporary staff' (Penelope Fitzgerald, 1980); 'The UN . . . does have machinery designed to . . . keep the peace among nations' (*Christian Science Monitor*, 1987); (*among* now sounding slightly forced) 'A conversation among Richard Smith, Sir Anthony Grabham, and Professor Cyril Chantler' (*British Medical Journal*, 1989).

Traditionally, the types *between each* and *between every* followed by a singular noun have been firmly rejected in usage guides. The types 'there was a blackboard between each window' and 'a batsman who tried to gain time by blowing his nose between every ball' were corrected to 'there were blackboards between the windows' and '. . . after every ball'. But it is not difficult to track down historical evidence using the condemned constructions: 'Between each kiss her oaths of true loue swearing' (*The Passionate Pilgrime*, 1599); 'A row of flower-pots were ranged, with wide intervals between each pot' (Wilkie Collins, 1860); 'Staring at her furtively between each mouthful of soup' (Margaret Kennedy, 1924); 'Pausing between every sentence' (George Eliot, 1859).

Should we conclude that such *between each/every* constructions must now be accepted as part of standard English? Is it perverse to reject the historical evidence in support of 'between you and I' and accept it in the case of 'between every sentence'? I think not, but others may have a different view.

Sunday Times 3 June 1990

but

It should be said at the outset that *but* has many more normal than abnormal uses as an adversative conjunction and preposition: (conjunction) 'naughty but nice'; 'nature is cruel but tidy'; 'it was cool outside but even cooler inside'; 'the answer is not to remove the parish system but to put more resources into it'; (= except that) 'Claudia's eyes are closed but once or twice her lips twitch'; (preposition, = except (for)) 'the aftermath of the last economic crisis but one'; 'there is little to be seen but a forest of brick chimneys'. The examples, here and below, are all drawn from good sources.

But draw back from the regular adversative game and debates begin. First, the widespread public belief that *but* should not be used at the beginning of a sentence has no foundation but is seemingly unshakeable. In certain kinds of compound sentences (the *OED* says), *but* is used to introduce a balancing 'statement of the nature of an exception, objection, limitation, or contrast to what has gone before; sometimes, in its weakest form, merely expressing disconnection, or emphasizing the introduction of a distinct or independent fact'. A string of examples from the thirteenth century to the nineteenth is presented in the *OED*, including this one from the Authorized Version (1611): 'And went againe into the iudgement hall, & saith to Iesus, Whence art thou? But Iesus gaue him no answere' (John 19: 9). It should be said, though, that unless contextual dislocation is being deliberately sought as a rhetorical device, it is not desirable to litter the page with constructions like 'He is tired. But he is happy.'

Disagreement quickly arises about the case of pronouns (nouns, being without case distinction, are not affected) after *but* = except. Yards of comment and examples have been presented in the standard grammars about this problem. The most persuasive view now seems to be that when a *but*-construction lies within the subject area of a clause or sentence ('No one but she would dream of doing that') the subjective case is preferable; and when the *but*-construction lies within the object area ('No one else may use my typewriter but her') the objective case is desirable. The formula is not a watertight one. For example, when a subject containing *but* is delayed, but is merely an emphatic echo of the main subject, the case of the pronoun remains the same: 'But no one understood it, no one but I' (J. M. Coetzee, 1977). The simple formula is conspicuously broken in 'that was something no one remembered. No one but her, Lynnie thought' (Deborah Eisenberg, 1990).

But that (= except that, except for the fact that) constructions, and similar ones with omission of *that*, until recent times a cherished part of the literary language, now seem to be on a slow journey to extinction. The type is shown in: (*but that*) 'I too should be content to dwell in peace . . . But that my country calls' (Southey, 1795); 'I do not doubt but that you are surprised' (Ruskin, 1870); (*but* by itself) 'And but she spoke it dying, I would not Beleeue her lips' (Shakespeare's *Cymbeline*, 1611). It survives, however, in the formulaic 'It never rains but it pours'.

The type '*cannot but* + infinitive' has been in undisputed standard use since the sixteenth century: 'The frailty of man without thee cannot but fall' (*Book of Common Prayer*, 1549): 'I cannot but be gratified by the assurance' (Jefferson, 1812). If the verb *help*, however, happens to occur within the construction, usage guides start to put up warning signs (e.g. 'awkward and to be deprecated', Eric Partridge, 1942). Nevertheless the construction turns up regularly in the work of indisputably good writers: 'she could not help but follow him into the big department store' (Bernice Rubens, 1987); 'he could not help but admire Miss Leplastrier for the way she looked after the details' (Peter Carey, 1988). It is true that the construction is a combination of older ones, and that it is no more than a century old. The earliest example that anyone has found is this: 'She could not help but plague the lad' (Hall Caine, 1894).

Relative modernity can help to keep a construction from being frequently used in standard English. Tribalism is even more effective. One of the most surprising modern uses of *but* is its occurrence as a qualifying adverb at the end of sentences. Taking a lead from the Scots and the Irish, not-quite-standard speakers in Australia and in some parts of South Africa provide evidence of this construction which has not yet entered the English of England: 'Yes, I told 'im. Not the whole of it, but.' (David Malouf (Australia), 1985); 'That was a lovely cat, but.' (= that was a truly lovely cat) (Rajand Mesthrie (South Africa), 1987).

The smallest words in the language are never stationary.

Sunday Times 8 July 1990

compare

Spread all one's examples of the verb *compare* on the carpet, sort out which of them is construed with *to*, which with *with*, and which with no preposition at all, and why. A simple task, I thought, with very little room for differences of opinion.

For such an exercise, one can begin with Shakespeare's Sonnet 18: 'Shall I compare thee to a summer's day?' In it stress is placed on the likenesses, even though the loved one is declared to be 'more lovely and more temperate'. Or one can begin with the Song of Solomon (AV) 1: 9, 'I have compared thee, O my love, to a company of horses in Pharaoh's chariots'. As the *OED* expresses it, the meaning in both examples is 'to speak of or represent as similar, to liken'. With such patterns in mind, generations of speakers have continued to produce sentences in which the primary sense of *compare* is 'to liken'. Except that generations of churchgoers have regarded 'unto' as an admirable variant of 'to': 'For who in the heaven can be compared unto the Lord?' (Psalms 89: 6). In *Modern English Usage* Fowler's first rule (which I shall call Fowler's Proposition 1) was that the sentence 'He compared me *to* Demosthenes' means that 'he suggested that I was comparable to Demosthenes or put me in the same class'.

By contrast, 'He compared me *with* Demosthenes', according to Fowler, means that 'he instituted a detailed comparison or pointed out where and how far I resembled or failed to resemble him'. I shall call this Fowler's Proposition 2. It would appear to be supported by the following later example: 'He did not individually compare other women with her, but because she was the first, she was equal to his memory to the sum of all the others' (John Berger, 1972).

It seemed that two watertight rules had emerged. If it is simply a question of likening, use *to*. If the comparison is made in order to bring out both the likenesses and the differences, use *with*. Unfortunately, of the two propositions, only Proposition 1 now appears to be true.

As to the third class of constructions, there are plenty of sentences containing *compare* in which no preposition is called for: 'a randomised study was performed to compare two commonly adopted methods of seeking consent' (*British Medical Journal*, 1986).

Back to Proposition 2. The *OED* clearly regarded this proposition as unsound. Its sense 2 ('to mark or point out the similarities and differences of two or more things') allows for constructions using *either* 'with' or 'to': 'To compare Great things with small' (Milton, 1667); 'This cramping tendency of town as compared to country' (1879). To which may be added: 'Isabella then compared Angelo's judgement with God's judgement' (*English*, 1987); 'To compare NIVEs [= certain types of non-standard English] to other acquisitional phenomena is not to deny their legitimacy' (*English World-Wide*, 1987).

The battle is on. The *to*-users seem to dominate when a subordinate clause begins with the participial form *compared*; 'They taste gritty and dry now, compared to how they were' (Lee Smith, US writer, 1983); 'compared to Ward's witchhunters, Profumo is an almost blameless character in the story' (*London Review of Books*, 1987). But not always: 'The church looked dimly mysterious compared with the glare of the passage' (P. D. James, 1986).

There is one circumstance (we can call it Fowler's Proposition 3) in which the construction with *with* is obligatory, and this is when *compare* is used intransitively (*OED* sense 4b): 'This compares favourably with the inertness of England'; 'As athletes men cannot ... compare with horses or tigers or monkeys' (nineteenth-century examples in the *OED*); 'New York does not for a moment compare with Chicago' (William Archer, 1904). Or in such a sentence as 'His achievements do not compare with those of A. J. Ayer'.

Two possibly tangential points. There seems to be an overwhelming preference nowadays for *with* in the phrases '*by* (or *in*) comparison with', a preference which may have helped to build up the false belief that *compare*, too, should always be followed by *with*. It is of interest also to see how the translators of the New English Bible avoided *compare to* in almost every case in which it had been used in the Authorized Version: Isaiah 46: 5 (AV) 'To whom will ye liken me, and make me equal, and compare me?'; (NEB) 'To whom will you liken me? Who is my equal? With whom can you compare me?'; Proverbs 3: 15 (AV) 'all the things thou canst desire are not to be compared unto her'; (NEB) 'and all the jewels are no match for her'. The *to*-construction is retained only once. In the Song of Solomon passage mentioned above, the corresponding NEB sentence reads 'I would compare you, my dearest, to Pharaoh's chariot-horses'. Fowler's Proposition 1, I suppose.

Sunday Times 4 September 1988

dare

'Shall I part my hair behind? Do I dare to eat a peach?' (T. S. Eliot, 'The Love Song of J. Alfred Prufrock'). 'They dare not break in. They cannot break in' (T. S. Eliot, *Murder in the Cathedral*). These two contexts neatly show two quite different ways of using the verb *dare*. In the first it is an ordinary verb followed by a *to*-infinitive, and in the second it is a marginal modal (see below) followed by a negative and a bare (or plain) infinitive. They bring us to the heart of one of the subtlest and most variegated verbs in the language.

Grammarians use the term 'modal auxiliary' to describe the verbs *can/could*, *may/might*, *shall/should*, *will/would*, their abbreviated forms *'ll* and *'d*, and their contracted negative forms *can't*, *won't*, etc. One of the characteristic features of these is that none of them has a final *s* in the third person present indicative; we do not say *he cans*, *he mays*, *he shalls*, and so on. Four other verbs—*dare*, *need*, *ought to*, and *used to*—are called 'marginal modals' because their status is to some degree intermediate between that of modal auxiliaries and ordinary verbs. In Lord Alfred Douglas's famous line 'I am the Love that dare not speak its name', *dare*, with no final *s*, is a marginal modal.

The paradigm of this complex verb has had a chequered career. In Standard English only four elements survive in strength: *dare*, *dares*, *dared*, and *daring*. Technically *durst* also forms part of the verbal pattern, but the sequence of letters *D-u-r-s-t* is now much more likely to be a surname than the past tense (indicative or subjunctive) of the verb *dare*. In my recent reading I have encountered a few examples of *durst*, but only in historical, uneducated, dialectal, comic, or other special circumstances. 'He'll come all right. He ain't got nowhere to sleep, see. And I dursn't face him. He'll knock me about terrible' (Miss Read, *Village Affairs*); 'Though fain to avoid eavesdropping, he yet had durst not betray his presence' (Paul Jennings); 'Zounds! sirrah, how durst the Manhattan Punch Line attempt Sheridan's "Rivals"?' (*New York Times*, 1984). Each time I felt I had unearthed some very old or quaint linguistic bones.

In the earliest English records the main forms were *d(e)arr* (third person singular present indicative), *dorste/durste* (past tense), and *dorren* (past participle). These were joined in the sixteenth century by *dareth/dares* and by *dared* (as past tense and past participle).

The older forms gradually dropped out and now survive only in English regional dialects or in regional or substandard speech in the United States.

At the present time, there seem to be at least five main constructions in which *dare*, whether as a main verb or as a marginal modal, is used when followed by a bare infinitive. Most of them are negative or interrogative. (1) (subject + *dare* + negative) 'silences can only be masks for a tenderness he dare not show' (J. M. Coetzee). (2) (subject + auxiliary + negative + *dare*) 'Kennedy did not dare ask Congress for such a treaty' (*Daedalus*, 1986). (3) (subject + *dared* + negative) 'she dared not stir until eleven was safely past' (Ann Schlee). (4) (interrogative + *dare* + subject) 'How dare you come in without knocking!' (Roald Dahl). (5) (negative imperative auxiliary + *dare*) 'Don't you dare put that light on!' (Shelagh Delaney). Such uses together, according to my evidence, are three times as frequent as those in the following group.

Dare as a main verb followed by a *to*-infinitive is found in various negative, affirmative, and interrogative constructions: 'I did not dare to think what would happen if I failed' (Anita Brookner); 'None of Harvey's guests dared to speak' (Jeffrey Archer); 'How do they dare to be different?' (*New Yorker*, 1987).

Nowadays, because of its double status as an ordinary verb and as a marginal modal, *dare* can be used without inflection, for past as well as present time: (present) 'a person hardly dare think in this house'; (past) 'She turned round. She dare not look at his face.' The *OED* (in the relevant section which was published in 1894) condemned the past tense use as 'careless', and cited examples from the work of Frederick Marryat and Charles Kingsley among others. Modern grammarians regard it as unobjectionable.

I cannot list here all the delicious regional forms of the verb—*daur, dussn't, darst 'ee*, and so on. Nor have I space to deal with the types 'I dare (= challenge, defy) you to contradict me', and 'I dare say' (= venture to say, presume to say). They have a history of their own. There is a great deal more to this busy little word than I have described, but, as an American might say, 'I dasn't go on'.

Sunday Times 7 August 1988

designer

A designer is, of course, one who designs. First recorded in 1649, the word has tended to drift in three main directions, more or less following the lead of the verb from which it is derived. First, from the beginning, it has had the simple and obvious sense 'one who originates a plan or plans'. A monarch, a politician, a philosopher, anyone with a grand design, qualified for the label designer. God could be and was seen as the Great Designer.

But plans and designs can go awry or be intentionally or primarily evil: the *OED* records examples of designers who were 'plotters and lifters up of themselves against the interest of Christ'. A writer in 1726 is quoted as asking, 'Where is one faithful friend to be chosen out among a thousand base designers?'

The third type of designer also emerged in the seventeenth century: one who makes an artistic design or plan of construction, as the *OED* expresses it. Such people traditionally made preliminary sketches for pictures or other works of art, or outlines of any pieces of decorative art. As time moved on the word was applied to draughtsmen who made plans for manufacturers or architects, for people who designed clothes, and for those who designed sets for stage and other dramatic performances.

All this is commonplace and all three senses are well documented in dictionaries and other works of reference.

Then something happened. In the 1960s the word (and society) moved into significantly new territory. 'Designer' began to be applied to fashionable clothing bearing the name or label of famous designers, with the implication that the garments were more stylish, better designed, by people who knew their craft.

Designer scarves were announced in American newspapers in 1966. A decade later Mrs Jimmy Carter, good Democrat as ever, was reported by the *Washington Post* as 'rejecting anything she feels inflated by designer labels'. By contrast, good Republicans were presumably going overboard for designer items. Designer sheets, pillowcases, furniture, make-up, dresses, blouses, jeans, stormed into the catalogues, especially designer jeans. The *Washington Post* reported in 1978 that 'designer jeans are such big business that Bloomingdale's has created a department called "Pure Jeanius"'. Thomas Green, Ford's US custom-car marketing manager, told the *New York Times* that 'about 26 percent of the total Mark V's in 1979 are designer cars'. Many classes of society, first in America, and then in Britain and elsewhere, came to love or loathe designer labels and designer collections.

The craze branched out. In 1984 *The Times* reported someone as saying 'Small wonder Perrier is called Designer Water. My local wine bar has the cheek to charge 70p a glass.' By 1986 the periodical *Annabel* was describing designer stubble as the macho image, and showing Bob Geldofic faces with two-day (or longer) growths. Designer drugs began to appear, that is drugs subtly altered from illegal substances already on the market in such a way that addicts were able to enter perilous psychedelic territory without breaking the law. Some rich Californian hippies were reported as looking for designer gods, their other sources of meditational satisfaction given up as failures. The Labour Party was declared by the media to be flirting with designer socialism, once it had dawned on Neil Kinnock and his senior colleagues that the older kind of socialism was no longer a winning ticket.

During the Olympic Games this year it seems that forged brand-name clothes and watches were easily obtainable in Seoul. *The Times* reported that 'many competitors had bought forged Fila shirts, which have two designer marks to show how prestigious they are'.

The word *designer*, employed to indicate expense or rarity, or something exclusive or special, looks like staying around for a while—obviously in the world of fashion with the likes of Giorgio Armani's black label, but further afield too. Douglas Hurd, the Home Secretary, echoing a recent attack by the Prince of Wales on 'the incessant menu of utterly gratuitous violence' in films and on television, attacked 'designer violence' on the screen. At least one local authority has jumped to attention: the residents of Notting Hill, West London, have been promised 'designer crime-free streets'. Even the TUC at its 1988 conference displayed a giant slogan ('*Your* union is working for *you*') at Bournemouth, painted in what the *Spectator* described as 'the sort of designer colours (pink, grey and orange) which are nowadays associated . . . with the New Realism'.

As an adjective, *designer* is swerving about as vogue words tend to. The next thing, I suppose, to judge from the Porter scene in this year's Stratford production of *Macbeth*, will be designer comedy. At the performance I saw, the Porter, swaggering about the stage and ogling the audience, asked in a leering voice, 'Knock, knock! Who's there? (*pause*) Duncan? (*another pause*) Dunk and disorderly.'

For all I know this unShakespearian throwaway line may have been adlibbed on the day. At all events the audience loved it.

Sunday Times 6 November 1988

do

Put aside regional uses and illiteracies like 'I never done anybody any harm' and there remain a multitude of ways in which the verb *do* operates as one of the busiest words in the language. One must first distinguish its use as a full verb with multiple meanings from its use as an auxiliary. In practice it is used as a main verb much less frequently—the proportions vary from book to book but are of the order of 1 : 10—than it is used as an auxiliary. Examples of its use as a main verb: 'we used to do most things together' (= carry out, perform); 'anything will do' (= suffice); 'I just brought you an article I've done' (= written); 'I wanted to bring them up to do you proud' (idiom). Somehow we acquire and more or less master several dozen such uses, all of them clearly differentiated.

Do used as an auxiliary is a much more complicated matter, though paradoxically it seems always to fall into place without any particular difficulty. In the categories that follow, unless otherwise specified, all the examples are drawn from two novels that I happen to be reading at the moment, André Brink's *States of Emergency* (1988) and Anita Brookner's *Lewis Percy* (1989), but they could have been drawn from almost anywhere. Some of the main types: (1) (In interrogative and negative contexts followed by a plain infinitive) 'Did I somehow dread the prospect of returning?'; 'Do you realize this is the first time you've ever told me anything about yourself?'; 'I didn't know (still don't) how to cope with the fact'; (with uncontracted negative) 'But does not the fate of her small novella demonstrate the futility of such an enterprise?' (2) (In affirmative, including imperative, statements, with varying degrees of emphasis) 'It really did seem as if a better world could still come about'; 'if you do choose me it is a different me you'll have to contend with in future'; 'But do remember, won't you, that we live rather a long way away.' (3) (= *haven't got*, a construction associated with America but now widespread) 'Bathrooms in the bedrooms. Cocktail bars. Things we don't have'—Anthony Lejeune, 1986; 'we don't have that kind of thing in my house, man'—Brink, 1988; 'I don't have any standards myself'—Brookner, 1989. (4)

(With inversion of subject in various circumstances) 'Only after what seems to be hours . . . do they manage to shake off their pursuers'; 'Such arrested innocence affected him painfully, as did her large eyes'; 'So anxious did this make him that he was determined never to court such condemnation again.' (5) (In tag questions) 'And when you and I talk about history we don't mean what actually happened, do we?'—Penelope Lively, 1987; 'You like Pen, don't you?'—Brookner, 1989; 'Yet I knew you at once, didn't I?'—Brookner, 1989. (6) (Substitutive *do*; also, on occasion, *do so*, i.e. contexts in which *do* or *do so* refer back to the predicate of a preceding clause) 'who had married the ungenerous Susan because that was what men did'; 'she might have spent pleasant harmless days, as women of her generation were accustomed to do'; 'So he gave her a coin and playfully instructed her to telephone him the day she turned eighteen. Which, against all odds, she did'; if that meant accepting George . . . he was perfectly willing to do so'; 'Yet this marriage was by now so established that he had no choice but to continue it. There was no good reason not to do so.'

Two subsidiary points are worth noting. First, the contracted forms *don't*, *didn't*, and *doesn't*, none of which was recorded in print before the later part of the seventeenth century, are now customary in the representation of speech, but by convention are still hardly ever used in ordinary descriptive prose. Examples: (in conversations) ' "Doesn't she ever go out them?" asked Lewis'; 'Why don't you do that?'; 'I didn't know what could have happened to you'; (uncontracted) 'He did not think he could tell her about the stunning monotony of his everyday life'; 'What she lived on Lewis never knew, but money did not appear to be a problem'; 'the story I should like to write does not allow me to focus only on itself'.

Secondly, nowadays it passes almost without notice that in the phrase 'I don't think' the negativity has often been 'illogically' transferred from where it 'properly' applies: 'I don't think I've ever met anyone like you' (= I think I have never, etc.); 'The youth honestly didn't think Vuyani would survive his detention'; 'I don't think he likes to be teased'. In each case the subject *is* thinking, and the negativity belongs in what follows. The monarchs of usage used to complain, but the migration of the negativity in such circumstances is now irreversible.

Sunday Times 6 January 1991

garbage

'Numbers Ten and Eleven Downing Street are no longer lobbing garbage across the metaphorical fence and turning up the ghetto-blaster at next door's bedtime'—Robin Oakley in *The Times* earlier this year.

The sentence leads naturally to a consideration of how the predominantly American word *garbage* (in its literal sense) has come to be largely restricted in Britain to ideas and opinions that are, or are considered to be, of no value or importance. What the dustman collects in Britain is not garbage, but rubbish, refuse, or domestic waste.

First, a word about origins. The etymology of the word *garbage* (and also of the word *trash*) is unknown. *Garbage* was at first (from about 1430) used to mean the offal of an animal used as food. By the late sixteenth century it was being used for refuse in general. In the mid-sixteenth century, *trash* began to be used for lopped-off twigs or branches, and at the beginning of the eighteenth century for sugar-cane left over after the removal of its juice. In the course of the sixteenth century the word began to be applied to anything of little value, material or immaterial. Its most famous use is in Shakespeare's *Othello*, 'Who steales my purse, steales trash'.

Back to *garbage*. There is no doubt that *garbage* is the dominant word in the United States for the richer, stenchier, vaporous stuff—vegetable peelings, leftover food, scraps, that sort of thing. Americans tend to distinguish it from *trash*, which is predominantly the flimsier sort of discarded material thrown into the wastepaper basket (*wastebasket* in the US)—letters, especially junk mail, newspapers, used Kleenex, broken toys, and so on, 'the remnants of our private and public lives', as an American professor expressed it recently. The two words overlap considerably: 'Du Page County *garbage* would get a one-way ticket out of town under a proposal to ship the *trash* to a small Downstate city' (*Chicago Sun-Times*, 1988). Spreadeagled across the border between *garbage* and *trash* are empty plastic bottles, discarded paint brushes, old bath mats, and every other smallish kind of throw-out.

Modern processes of recycling have brought alternating connotations of pleasure and despair to the concept of waste material. The state of New Jersey, for instance, has passed a law making recycling mandatory across the state. Anything that can be recycled must be placed in distinguishable garbage or trash bags or cans. Non-biodegradable objects are to be separately bagged or displayed. But there is no sign that the words *garbage* and *trash* will neatly fall into line to signify biodegradable and non-biodegradable matter respectively. The language cannot be regimented in this way even if the waste can.

Rubbish vans (or rear end-loading garbage trucks, trash compactors, garbage compactors, refuse collection vehicles, and whatever else they are called in the US) continue to pick up garbage containers in American streets. But before they arrive the bags and bins, as everywhere, are readily accessible to animals, scavengers, vagrants —and the police. A Supreme Court ruling in America earlier this year ruled that refuse left out for collection 'for the express purpose of conveying it to a third party, the trash collector' may be searched by the police for incriminating evidence (drugs, for example) without a warrant. Garbage on the street is no longer private property.

A professor at the University of Arizona, William Rathje, has earned himself a place in sociological textbooks by studying garbage for its 'societal meaning'. The garbage is 'logged into 185 categories', and the subject is called *garbology*. It is difficult to see why discarded styrofoam hamburger packages have any independent value for sociology beyond that observable at the point of purchase.

Back to Britain. Local dustmen (a word first recorded in 1707) continue to empty our dustbins (a word first recorded in Dickens's *Dombey and Son* in 1848) and take away the black or green plastic bags in which we have placed our rubbish. *Garbage* is chiefly in figurative use, of nonsensical or rubbishy views, whether written or spoken, but also in that boring computer adage 'Garbage in, garbage out' (poor input produces worthless output).

Let me end on a personal note. In 1986 a black cab-driver in Washington who was driving me to the Library of Congress where I was to make a speech about the completion of *A Supplement to the OED* told me that he thought the Oxford Dictionary was the best dictionary in the world. 'You know, the one with the microscope' (he meant the magnifying glass), he said. 'Did you get your copy from the Book of the Month Club?' I asked. 'The Book of the *what* Club?' he retorted. 'No, I found it in the trash.'

Sunday Times 21 August 1988

Comment from a reader. 'Using and manufacturing styrofoam is a sociopathic activity (like driving a car), and the masses, in which one can include Royalty and the President of MacDonald's International, are unwilling to see or acknowledge the long-term destructive effect which the total product, its manufacture, and the chemicals in it have for the environment. In the case of styrofoam, not only might it have an "independent value for sociology", but also for biochemistry, meteorology (ozone), and geology (it is non-compactible), to name only a smattering of the individual sciences.' (J. Dingeman, private letter of 23 August 1988)

help

'Once, during a snowstorm, he helped me dig out my driveway.' This sentence in a recent issue of the *New Yorker* leads to a grammatical question: which form of the infinitive is customary or which is desirable after the verb *help*—a *to*-infinitive or a bare infinitive? A bare infinitive is, of course, one not preceded by the particle *to*. Should the sentence have read '. . . he helped me *to* dig out my driveway?'

To try to see what governs the matter, one must go back to the beginnings of the construction. After the Norman Conquest the verb *help* normally governed an infinitive with *to*: (with infinitive alone) 'Theodorus . . . halp [helped] to putte Wilfredus out of his bisshopricke' (John of Trevisa, 1387); (with object and infinitive) 'Or help other men to sing' (*Cursor Mundi*, written about 1300). Occasionally in Middle English, and more commonly from the sixteenth century onward, *help* was also followed by a bare infinitive: 'I wol thee helpe hem carie' (Chaucer's *Pardoner's Tale*); 'to helpe garnishe his mother tongue' (Nicholas Udall, 1548); 'Many helpfull men That . . . would then Helpe beare his mighty seven-fold shield' (Chapman's translation of the *Iliad*, about 1611).

Shakespeare used both constructions: 'and help to celebrate A contract of true love' (*The Tempest*); 'Sirs, help our uncle to convey him in' (*Titus Andronicus*); 'that I should wish for thee to help me curse . . . that foul bunch-backed toad' (*Richard III*); 'I must woo you To help unarm our Hector' (*Troilus & Cressida*). In his work the construction with the *to*-infinitive is about six times as common as that with the bare infinitive. Other Elizabethan and Jacobean writers also used both constructions after *help*. Thus from Marlowe's *Tamburlaine* (1586–7): 'For they are friends that help to wean my state'; 'And here's the crown, my lord; help set it on.'

Voyages of discovery and settlement took English speakers abroad from the Elizabethan period onward. Circumstances changed. The verb *help* moved into different linguistic climates and its distributional patterns changed.

The general pattern now, in the late 1980s, seems to be something like this. (1) The construction with a *to*-infinitive appears to be the more usual one in Standard English: 'where he helped to look after German prisoners of war' (*British Medical Journal*, 1986); 'a well-designed phonics system helps most children to read well' (*Daily Telegraph*, 1987). But the construction with bare infinitive also occurs: 'Our every deed must help make us acceptable' (*The Times*, 1986); 'It helped silence critics on the party left' (Kenneth O. Morgan, 1987). It is not altogether clear what governs the choice.

(2) By contrast, in American English and also in Australia, New Zealand, and South Africa, the form with the bare infinitive predominates. Examples: 'I had helped her carry it to her bedroom' (Garrison Keillor, 1986, USA); 'in the hope that this may help provoke a transformation' (*New Yorker*, 1986); 'she made me help her catch a young turkey' (Marian Eldridge, 1984, Australian); 'Mandy helped him choose something for Claire' (C. K. Stead, 1986, NZ); 'the labourers' training school he helped create' (*Highveld Style*, 1986, South African). But the construction with a *to*-infinitive is also found in these areas often enough: 'It may help us to conceive of their predicament if we imagine . . .' (*Daedalus*, 1986, US); 'The levees were helping to aggravate the problem they were meant to solve' (*New Yorker*, 1987).

(3) One governing factor, past and present, and in all present-day varieties of English, is a natural reluctance to adopt the sequence *to help* + a *to*-infinitive, that is, to repeat *to*. The construction does occur ('she allowed Pearl to help her to stack up her hair'—Iris Murdoch, 1983), but it is not common. In this respect it is noteworthy that Shakespeare's examples of *help* + a bare infinitive occur only when the verb *help* is itself preceded by the particle *to*. This reluctance to repeat *to* may partially account for some of the American and Antipodean occurrences of the construction with the bare infinitive: 'One of my housemates . . . offered to help me move in' (*New Yorker*, 1986); 'she had moved heaven and earth to help me win the Scholarship to Oxford' (the athlete Jack Lovelock, as reported in a recent biography). But this is not certain.

(4) One other circumstance is worth mentioning. In all areas, and

at all periods, if *help* is preceded by *cannot/can't but*, a bare infinitive is and was obligatory: 'the superficial parting they either meant to play or could not help but play' (*Shakespeare Quarterly*, 1985); 'she could not help but follow him into the big department store' (Bernice Rubens, 1987); 'Chattie can't help but agree' (Marian Eldridge, 1984). In fact the construction *cannot help but* + a bare infinitive has often been brought into question. Its critics say that it should give way to the type with a gerund and with *but* omitted ('Bertrand could not help venting his frustration upon Madeleine', Piers Paul Read, 1986). But that is another matter altogether.

Sunday Times 26 June 1988

like

Let us consider the use of *like* as a conjunction. In *Modern English Usage* Fowler cites this sentence from Charles Darwin (1866): 'Unfortunately few have observed like you have done.' The Great Schoolmaster's view of the construction was expressed with characteristic verve: 'Every illiterate person uses this construction daily; it is the established way of putting the thing among all who have not been taught to avoid it; the substitution of *as* for *like* in their sentences would sound artificial. But in good writing this particular *like* is very rare.'

The *OED* (in a fascicle published in 1903) cited examples of *like* used as a conjunction from the works of Shakespeare, Southey, William Morris, Jerome K. Jerome, and others, and added the comment: 'Now generally condemned as vulgar or slovenly, though examples may be found in many recent writers of standing.'

The status of conjunctional *like* has been debated many times since then. The most recent authority, *A Comprehensive Grammar of the English Language* (1985), slightly disguises the problem by speaking of 'clausal adjuncts' and 'semantically equivalent phrasal adjuncts', but the verdict is nevertheless much as before. Constructions like 'Please try to write as I do' and 'Please try to write like me' are standard; but 'Please try to write like I do' is described as being only in informal use, and especially in American English.

Thus, throughout the present century, the mood has been condemnatory. The use of *like* as a conjunction has been dismissed as 'illiterate', 'vulgar', 'sloppy', or, in the modern coded language of grammarians, 'informal'. Evelyn Waugh spoke for his generation of writers, and for many people still, when he said of Henry Green's *Pack My Bag* (1940) 'Only one thing disconcerted me . . . The proletarian grammar—the "likes" for "ases", the "bikes" for "bicycles", etc.'

I have reconsidered the matter by examining the works of 'many recent writers of standing', British, American, and from further afield, and the results are, I think, of interest. After I had set aside some really lazy sentences, four main conjunctional uses of *like* emerged.

First, quite frequently, with repetition of the verb used in the main clause, and bearing the sense 'in the way that': 'They didn't talk like other people talked' (Martin Amis, 1981); 'Gordon needs Sylvia like some people need to spend an hour or two every day simply staring out of the window' (Penelope Lively, 1987); 'I'm afraid it might happen to my baby like it happened to Jefferson' (*New Yorker*, 1987). This use, which owes something to the song 'If you knew Susie like I know Susie', is common in all English-speaking countries, and must surely escape further censure or reproach. Naturally, though, we may continue to use other constructions if we wish to, and in good company: 'She changed wallpapers and lampshades the way some women changed their underwear' (A. N. Wilson, 1986).

Secondly, it is frequently used in good American and Australian sources (though much less commonly in the UK) to mean 'as if, as though': 'It looks like it's still a fox' (*New Yorker*, 1986); 'She acts like she can't help it' (Lee Smith, 1987, American); 'I wanted him born and now it feels like I don't want him' (Elizabeth Jolley, 1985, Australian). One of the few British examples in my files is a sad one from BBC Radio 4 early in 1987: 'It looks like Terry Waite will leave for London in two or three hours.'

Thirdly, it is interchangeable with *as* in all English-speaking countries in a range of fixed, somewhat jocular, phrases of saying and telling: 'Send for your copy now. Like we said it's free' (*Globe & Mail*, Toronto, 1968); 'Like you say, you're a dead woman' (Mary Wesley, 1983); 'Well, like I told you, I work with him upstairs' (Peter Ackroyd, 1985); 'Like I said, I haven't seen Rudi for weeks' (Thomas Keneally, 1985); 'My whereabouts are in Merthyr Tydfil, like you said' (Bernice Rubens, 1985).

Fourthly, it is increasingly used, perhaps especially abroad, in contexts where a comparison is being made. In these it has the force of 'in the manner (that), in the way (that)': 'You call us Mum and Dad like you always have' (Mary Wesley, 1983); 'How was I to know she'd turn out like she did?' (Carolyn Burns, 1985, New Zealand); 'Like Jack and Jill came down the hill, Dilip also rolled down the box-office in "Karma"' (*Star & Style*, Bombay, 1986); 'The retsina flowed like the Arno did when it overflowed in 1966' (Taki, in the *Spectator*, 1987).

It would appear that in many kinds of written and spoken English *like* as a conjunction is struggling towards acceptable standard or neutral ground. It is not quite there yet. But the distributional patterns suggest that the long-standing resistance to this nippy little word is beginning to crumble as a new century approaches.

Sunday Times 20 March 1988

may/might

For more than twenty years writers in Britain, America, and elsewhere, despite distress signals put up by linguistic scholars, have used *may have* for *might have* in contexts, each of them expressing a hypothetical possibility, like the following: 'I am in no way blaming you for lacking the presence of mind to come to me earlier when I may have been able to do something about it' (the American novelist William Styron, 1968); 'It was useless to try nailing reinforcing timbers at sea, since this may have upset whatever fragile forces were holding the planking together' (*Sunday Times*, 1977); 'Had it not been for the media's willingness to report news of the charge in the sceptical terms they did, I may not have been acquitted' (Peter Hain, 1981); 'A mentally ill man may not have committed suicide had he been kept in hospital, rather than been discharged to be cared for in the community' (*Guardian*, 1990).

How has this use arisen when the sequence of tenses seems to be clearly wrong? Is there no clear-cut rule?

It is not difficult to find contexts in which *may have* and *might have* are treated as virtual equivalents. A news item in a recent issue of the *Oxford Times* began: 'Six prize-winning Shetland Ponies stolen from a field near Chalgrove may have been sold at Reading market'. The headline immediately above it read 'Stolen ponies might have been sold'. Perhaps the headline suggested a degree of tentativeness fractionally different from that in the text. But the context was not governed by presentness or pastness of tense.

There are headlines and headlines. Had the *Guardian* placed the headline 'Mentally ill man may not have committed suicide' above the sentence given above, the reader would not have been certain whether the person concerned had, or had not, committed suicide (he might, for argument's sake, have been murdered) until the text of the news item made it clear just what had happened.

There are other considerations. As modal auxiliaries, *may* and *might* have more than one function. Examine this pair of sentences: 'you may be wrong' (= it is possible/possibly/perhaps you are wrong); 'there might be a thunderstorm tonight' (= it is possible that . . .). In such contexts both *may* and *might* can be idiomatically used: *might* usually carries with it a slightly more marked degree of tentativeness.

What is beginning to emerge is that in certain circumstances *may* and *might* are interchangeable with only slight change of focus or emphasis. It is not always a rigorous matter of contrasting tenses, much more a question of judging the degree of hypothetical possibility.

Consider further the interchangeability of *could* and *might* in the following pair of sentences: 'There could be a storm when the council's decision becomes known'; and 'Of course, I might be wrong.' Once more, *might* seems to provide a slightly greater degree of uncertainty.

May and *might*, as modal auxiliaries, have another function altogether, when they are used in contexts of permission. Examples: 'You may have another piece of cake if you wish'; (a somewhat old-fashioned use) 'Might I ask when the library opens?' Used thus, *may* is more formal and less common than another modal, namely *can*, and is also distinctly more common than *might*.

Longman's *Comprehensive Grammar of the English Language* (1985) recognizes the problem described in my first paragraph, but relegates it to a footnote: 'There is a tendency for the difference between *may* and *might* (in a sense of tentative or hypothetical possibility) to become neutralized. Thus some speakers perceive little or no difference of meaning between "You may be wrong" and "You might be wrong". This neutralization occasionally extends, analogically, to contexts in which only *might* would normally be considered appropriate: e.g. "An earlier launch of the lifeboat *may* [= might] *have averted* the tragedy." The fact that sentences such as this occasionally occur is a symptom of a continuing tendency to erode the distinctions between real and unreal senses of the modals.'

My various correspondents, as well as scholars who have written on the matter, especially S. F. Whitaker and Dwight Bolinger in 1987 and 1988 issues of the journal *English Today*, would doubtless have preferred the subject to have been thrashed out more thoroughly in the *Comprehensive Grammar* with more substantial evidence provided. There is much more to be said about *may* and *might* than I have room for here. But in my view, in the sentences cited in my first paragraph, *may have* is wrong. Taking all considerations into account, reality and unreality, the degree of the hypothetical possibilities, and the sequence of tenses, *might have* is required in each case, though I can see how easy it is to confuse the roles of *may* and *might* when in some circumstances they are more or less interchangeable.

Sunday Times 2 September 1990

prevent

Jonathon Porritt concluded an article on Green politics in a recent issue of the *Listener* by saying: 'Be that as it may, the Government now has an enormous challenge on its hands if it is to prevent its new environmental awareness backfiring in its face.' Should he perhaps have written 'to prevent its new environmental awareness *from* backfiring in its face'? What, if anything, governs the presence or absence of *from* in constructions of the type *prevent* + object (+ *from*) + *-ing*?

Both types came into existence at about the same time: (Type 1) 'Any Expedient . . . for preventing ffurther heats arriseing vpon such occasions' (*Colonial Records of Pennyslvania*, 1689); (Type 2) 'So great a number of troops . . . as should be able to . . . prevent the enemy from erecting their magazines' (Swift, 1711). In the eighteenth and nineteenth centuries no clear-cut UK/US distinction is detectable. The choice seems to have been governed by the rhythm or general run of the sentence rather than by any formal rules or by geographical distribution.

The object between the verb *prevent* and the *-ing* form is frequently a simple pronoun. To account for the variation found in such constructions, the *OED* says that '*Prevent me going* appears to be short for *prevent me from going*, perhaps influenced by *prevent my going*'. Very likely, despite the fact that the construction with a possessive pronoun (which I shall call Type 3) is not recorded before 1841.

I have pursued the three constructions in the English of the main English-speaking regions and found that new patterns have emerged and are beginning to settle in various areas. The Britishness of Type 1 is unmistakable: 'Your absurd behaviour will prevent me coming here any more' (Conrad, 1912); 'The only way the Government can prevent us taking part [in the Olympic Games] is by taking away the passports of all our competitors' (Sir Dennis Follows, 1980); 'its chained library of 1500 volumes dating back to the ninth century, chained up to prevent them from being nicked' (*The Times*, 1985). By contrast, a recent usage guide from America, Bryan A. Garner's *Dictionary of American Legal Usage* (1987), says that '*prevent* nowadays [in the US] ordinarily takes *from*, although archaically it is used with a direct object and a gerund'.

Type 2 is found in all areas: 'Those two considerations . . . prevented Hegst . . . from going away' (Conrad, 1915); 'it was only loyalty to Augustus and Livia that prevented him from spitting at me' (Robert Graves, 1934); 'Sleeman had tried to prevent a widow from committing suttee' (Ruth Prawer Jhabvala, 1975); 'I . . . failed to prevent Braimoh and Aina his wife from abandoning their matrimonial bed to me' (Chinua Achebe, 1987); 'Something seemed to be preventing him from looking her in the eye' (Kingsley Amis, 1988).

Type 3 (employing a possessive pronoun) seems to be in swift retreat, though not everyone thinks so: 'I shall prevent his learning Latin' (Penelope Fitzgerald, 1986); 'But even this does not prevent his being a fool' (Saul Bellow, 1987). Longman's *Comprehensive Grammar of the English Language* (1985) expresses it this way: 'the genitive form of the subject [= the type 'I dislike his driving my car'] is an option in formal English, but is often felt to be awkward or stilted'.

The verb *prevent* is not the only one governing an *-ing* clause optionally led by *from*. In various circumstances, and in particular when used in the broad sense 'restrain, prevent', the verbs *hinder*, *keep*, *prohibit*, and *stop* present the same choice. In the case of *stop*, the transatlantic divide is most marked. The older construction with *from* ('What can be done to stop him from running headlong on ruin'—Walter Scott, 1816) seems to have largely vanished from Standard English: 'I wish you would stop him circulating those rumours' (1917 in *OED*); 'you still couldn't do anything to stop him throwing Jack out of the firm' (Kingsley Amis, 1988). By contrast, *Webster's Third New International Dictionary* lists only constructions with *from* to illustrate the same use ('pleaded with him to stop him from resigning'; 'stopped him from making a speech that would have ruined him'). Also from North America: 'they were going to the whore-house to stop George from selling Daniel's grand-daughters' (D. A. Richards, 1981, Canadian). I believe that both the *from* and the *from*-less construction can still be used both in North America and in Britain, but the two varieties of English seem to be moving slowly in opposite directions in the matter.

The possibility that something different is happening to -*ing* constructions across the water is reinforced by the fate of the construction *keep* (in the intransitive sense 'to restrain or contain oneself from') + an -*ing* clause. The *OED* records the use from Charlotte Yonge's *Cameos* (1877): 'Nor was Louis able to keep from turning pale'. This use now sounds distinctly archaic. In American English, on the other hand, the construction flourishes: 'Maria cut the wheel to the left, to keep from hitting the cans' (Tom Wolfe, 1987); 'Nathan pulled upward on the frazzled leg of his shorts and tried to keep from crying (*New Yorker*, 1988). I cannot keep from thinking that such things are continuing to prise the two forms of English apart.

Sunday Times 11 June 1989

Comments from a reader: 'As one who is much concerned with editing both English and American copy, I was particularly interested in the transatlantic distinctions you drew. But I was a little puzzled by a couple of them, and wondered if you had not perhaps overlooked slight distinctions of meaning.

Would I, for example, be entirely mistaken in thinking that, if I wrote "He tried to stop me from reading your article" it meant that he had aimed to prevent me (from reading it) whereas "He tried to stop me reading your article" might carry the implication that he endeavoured to snatch it from me in the act of reading?

Further, if Tom Wolfe had written "Maria cut the wheel to the left, to keep hitting the cans", surely he would have been saying precisely the opposite from what he actually said? I don't really find the Charlotte Yonge usage archaic-sounding, as "nor was Louis able to keep turning pale" means something entirely different, if anything at all.' (Private letter from Stanley Sadie, editor of *The New Grove Dictionary of Music & Musicians*, 19 June 1989)

From my reply (29 June 1989): 'I agree that there is a possible threat of snatching in the sentence "He tried to stop me reading your article", but in the examples I have so far collected from British and North American sources the choice is normally a formal grammatical one (i.e. the presence or absence of *from*), not governed by differences of meaning.

I agree that the omission of *from* in the Charlotte Yonge and Tom Wolfe contexts would effectively reverse the sense. But my point was, rather, that "*keep from* + gerund" is no longer a customary construction in British English. It looks as if you might not agree with me.'

try and/to

Arguments continue to rage about the validity of *try and* followed by an infinitive instead of *try to*. Eric Partridge (1942) described *try and* as 'an astonishingly frequent error'. A recent Australian usage guide (1987) by Stephen Murray-Smith is just as severe: 'There is no doubt that "You must try and do it" is grammatically wrong, and is certainly not acceptable in written English.' Fowler's judgement was much more lenient in 1926. After briefly setting out the facts he concluded: '*try and* is an idiom that should not be discountenanced, but used when it comes natural'. He went on to make out a sort of case for the semantic distinctiveness of *try and* constructions.

In 1983, a Scandinavian scholar, Åge Lind, examined a group of fifty modern English novels of the period 1960–70 and found that *try to* was likely to occur in certain syntactic conditions, *try and* in others, and that in some circumstances the choice seemed not to be governed by any particular reason. 'If a subtle semantic distinction exists it does not seem to be observed,' he concluded.

Over the last three years I have gathered a wide range of evidence, with the following results. First, whatever the cause, in all manner of writing, *try to* is the more frequent of the two in the proportion of 3 : 1.

Standard examples of *try to* occurred in a wide range of constructions: (preceded by an auxiliary verb) 'I think we should try to help him as a family' (Iris Murdoch, 1983); (preceded by the infinitive marker *to*) 'To try to forget is to try to conceal' (T. S. Eliot, 1950); 'Mr Stratton's moods would always be a mystery, so much so that he had ceased to try to fathom them' (Peter Carey, 1988); (preceded by an adverb) 'I always try to travel light' (Robert Elms, 1988); (separated from the infinitive it governs) 'He's gone his own way, I go mine, or try to' (Kathy Page, 1989).

Parallel examples of *try and* for all but the last type are not difficult to find: (preceded by an auxiliary verb) 'We must try and find him at once' (J. R. R. Tolkien, 1954); 'I will try and answer any questions you may have' (Susan Hockey, University of Oxford lecture, 1981); (preceded by the infinitive marker *to*) 'he used to try and draw Dr De Wet out' (Menán du Plessis, 1983); (preceded by an adverb) 'He proceeded to just try and talk me out of it' (Diane Vaughan, 1986). Some other examples are less easy to classify: 'They will have to try and find out whose shop it is' (Dalene Matthee, 1986); 'he glanced at her face to try and see if she was mollified' (Piers Paul Read, 1986); 'I try and work on the assumption that they're all as smart as I am' (Clive James, 1987). Observe that some of these examples are drawn from the informal atmosphere of a lecture room or a newspaper interview, or from non-British sources. *Try and* can also occur idiomatically in the imperative in such sentences as 'Don't try and frighten me' (which, as it happens, is to be found in Thackeray's *Vanity Fair*, 1847).

It is only when one turns to other parts of the verb (i.e. *tries, tried, trying*) that a gulf between the two expressions opens up. Try to substitute *tries and* (etc.) for *tries to* (etc.) in the following examples, and the impossibility of it all becomes apparent: 'He tries to centre his mind on that sound' (C. K. Stead, 1984); 'I . . . paced around and tried to absorb all the details' (Anita Brookner, 1986); 'Einar tried to coach us in semaphore signals' (Garrison Keillor, 1986); 'as if trying to guess what her answer should be' (Piers Paul Read, 1986).

Try and gains a small amount of additional currency, perhaps, from the use of *and* to connect two verbs 'the latter of which would logically be in the infinitive' (as the *OED* expresses it). The commonest of such verbs are *come* ('You will come and see us sometimes, won't you?') and *go* ('Do go and thank him'). These two verbs, however, have no past or present tense restrictions. Clearly it is idiomatic to say 'You came and saw me yesterday' and 'He went and thanked him last week'. So the parallel with *try and* is far from exact.

Sunday Times 11 November 1990

want

The verb *want* has twenty-nine senses and sub-senses listed in the *OED*, divided into six main groups. Of these twenty-nine, thirteen are shown to have dropped out of use at various times since the word first entered the language from Old Norse round about 1200, and one, recorded only in Shakespeare's *Macbeth* ('who cannot want the thought?' = who can help thinking?), is shown the red card by being labelled 'Confused use'. Such a rate of loss suggests that the language has been intolerant whenever this non-native verb looked like threatening the territory of other verbs of strong presence, especially *lack, need, desire,* and *wish.*

Lost constructions include *it wants of six (o'clock)* = it is not quite six (1709 in *OED*); *something wants* (followed by *to* + infinitive) = something is lacking ('Then, shall I see Laurentum in a flame, Which only wanted to compleat my shame'—Dryden, 1697); and *to want of* = to lack, not to have ('Unwrought gold and silver want considerably of that lustre and brightness they appear in at goldsmiths' shops'—George Smith, 1799). For some six centuries the verb *want* was welcomed into the whole of the linguistic space containing the *intransitive* notion of 'to be lacking or missing or being deficient in some respect'. Then the curtain began to come down.

Transitive uses have fared better over the centuries: e.g. (= not to have) 'A purely optimistic creed always wants any real stamina' (Leslie Stephen, 1876); (in Palaeography and Bibliography) 'folio i8 wants 1 leaf) (*Anglo-Saxon England*, 1976); (= to come short of in telling the time of day) 'It only wants five minutes to dinner' (Trollope, 1865). Even these uses, however, now sound distinctly antiquated, and some of them have retreated into dialectal use. A Scottish use of *wanting* (present participle) meaning 'not having' is shown in Stevenson's *Kidnapped* (1886): 'I would not go wanting [= without] sword and gun'.

Want still holds its own in the battle with *need* in the idiomatic phrase *to want for nothing,* in advertisements (e.g. 'Wanted, a receptionist'; 'Wanted, early books written on Fiji'), elliptically for 'Wanted by the police', and in a few other circumstances. But it is on the retreat.

The notion of lacking or needing leads easily enough to the notion of desiring or wishing to have, but such uses, though now routine—indeed dominant—are relatively recent. The *OED*'s earliest examples date from the early eighteenth century, just at the time when the verb was shedding its traditional sense of 'lacking'. Typical examples: 'If every one of your clients is to force us to keep a clerk, whether we want to or not, [etc.]' (Dickens, 1840); 'I want you to be a good boy' (Sylvester Judd, 1845). This branch of meaning, the 'wishing' branch, firmly established itself in the nineteenth century and is now the dominant sense of the verb.

Current idiomatic applications include 'to wish for the possession of' (e.g. 'Thomas wants a word processor for Christmas'), and 'to need a person sexually'. There are also two somewhat non-standard uses of the verb in place of *need*: (1) *want* + gerund ('David thought he wanted helping into bed'—Marilyn Duckworth, 1960); 'Well, this Perlmutter wants locking up for a start'—Kingsley Amis, 1988). (2) *want* + infinitive ('you want to pull yourself together' (= you need to, you must)).

New uses of the verb are arriving all the time. Modern uses, some of them not yet registered in the *OED* and other dictionaries, are shown in the following examples: (+ *that*-clause) 'You want that I should lose both my lieutenants together?' (Anthony Lejeune, 1986); (with ellipsis of a verb of motion, originally nineteenth-century Scottish) 'The Federal Reserve chairman Mr Paul Volcker has reportedly told friends that he wants out' (*Guardian*, 1984); (+ *for* + object clause, US only) 'My mother wanted so much for my sister to have the best animals' (*New Yorker*, 1989); (elliptical = do you want to?) ' "Want to try one?" I asked, without thinking' (Jean McGarry, 1990); (elliptical = want to) 'It means he will be able to come in whenever he wants' (Nigel Williams, 1985); ' "You can come in if you want," she says' (Beth Nugent, 1990); (= wish) 'I could do that if you want, but it may mean replacing a few strings' (Penelope Fitzgerald, 1980); 'So don't feel obliged to come along. Stay home if you want' (Fay Weldon, 1988); 'I'll meet you at Susan's party if you want' (Michael Bracewell, 1989).

The long battles between *want* and *lack* or *need* seem to be almost over. *Want* is not often wanted in such circumstances. Now *want* is threatening *want to* and *wish* in certain conditions. In our day-to-day life we pick our way among all the uses of *want* with reasonable consistency and certainty. How we acquire that certainty is deeply mysterious.

Sunday Times 2 December 1990

whereabouts

When the recent (May 1988) hijacking of the Kuwaiti jumbo jet ended at Algiers, one of the *Today* team on BBC Radio 4, in a summary of the news, said 'The whereabouts of the hijackers (*pause*) are unknown.' The pause drew attention to the grammatical uncertainty surrounding the word *whereabouts*. Supposing there had been only one hijacker, for instance, would the announcer have said 'His whereabouts *is* unknown'? What is the present status of this word?

It has had a long and fluctuating history. It started out in the form *whereabout* (with no final *s*) as an interrogative adverb ('Quar abute abide yee nu?'—*Cursor Mundi*, written about 1300). By the seventeenth century it was also being used as a noun. Shakespeare used the *s*-less form, the only spelling available at the time, once interrogatively ('I must not haue you henceforth, question me, Whether I go: nor reason where-about'—*1 Henry IV*), and once as a noun ('For feare The very stones prate of my where-about'—*Macbeth*). The form without final *s* survived long after Shakespeare, but only in a folkish and rural sort of way in the works of Lytton, Dickens ('my lady's whereabout'), Kipling, and some other writers. At the very end of the eighteenth century (*OED*'s first example is one of 1795) the now customary spelling *whereabouts* made its bow as a noun, and soon became the dominant form.

In passing, it is worth noting that it is not at all unusual in our roguish language for competing adverbs, with or without a final *s*, to survive side by side for centuries. As the *OED* remarks, 'beside every adverb in -*ward* there has always existed (at least potentially) a parallel formation in -*wards*, and vice versa'. Thus *afterward(s)*, *backward(s)*, *forward(s)*, *toward(s)*, and so on.

Words ending in -*about(s)* form rather a restricted group. Apart from *whereabout(s)*, the commonest ones are *hereabout(s)* and *thereabout(s)*. The *OED* also records *whenabouts* ('the time at which a thing happened') as a nonce-word in 1898, but nonce-words are by definition rarely repeated ghosts. Southey and one other writer used *whatabouts* as a noun in the sense 'what one is about, one's doings, one's occupations', and Nathaniel Hawthorne used *whatabout* in the same sense. But in each case the rare form is conjoined with *whereabouts*.

To return to *whereabouts*: standard authorities disagree about its status. Some say that, used as a noun, it can be construed either as a singular or as a plural. Others take a strong line, one way or the other. Knut Schibsbye (1970): '*Whereabouts* takes the singular.' Frederick T. Wood (1962): 'Even if the reference is to several persons, each with a different whereabouts, a singular verb is still used: "She has a brother and two sisters, but their whereabouts is unknown."' Tom McArthur (1981): '(only plural): "Her present whereabouts are not known."' A Polish professor of linguistics tells me that she was taught to use a plural verb after all uses of the word.

I cast about in all the sources available to me, and tendencies of a sort began to stand out. Of course there were plenty of unrevealing examples where the writer's view was left undetermined: 'The label does not reveal the whereabouts of the vineyard' (Paul Bailey, 1986); 'In Scotland . . . the erectors of signposts seem reluctant to reveal to the motorist the precise whereabouts of Dumfries' (Alice Thomas Ellis, 1988).

The sub-editors of American newspapers often make different choices when presenting the same story: 'Kuron said that two commission members, including Walensa, were free and that the whereabouts of two others was unknown' (*Los Angeles Times*); '. . . and the whereabouts of two others were not known' (*Washington Post*). Similarly, 'Dyson, whose whereabouts yesterday was not revealed by his staff' (*Washington Post*); '. . . the staff had been instructed to say Dyson's whereabouts were not known' (*New York Times*). In the context of the hijacking of the Kuwaiti plane, the *Financial Times* opted for a singular construction ('the whereabouts of the extremist Arab Shi'ites . . . was unclear last night'); and the *Los Angeles Times* similarly reported that 'the whereabouts of the hijackers remains unclear'. But in another recent issue of the *Los Angeles Times* there was an account of an axe-wielding rapist in Florida who had escaped and 'his present whereabouts are not known'.

Clearly the word *whereabouts* is tossing and turning in a number void, after two hundred years not yet ready to fit into a stipulated groove. I would like to say with confidence that a plural verb is preferable if the speaker has reason to believe that the persons or things spoken of are in different locations. By contrast, if the context is of (say) 'a young man and his companion' it would seem reasonable to turn to a singular form for the verb. But language is not reasonable or governable when choices are freely available, and *whereabouts* looks likely to remain an unfixed grammatical entity for some time to come.

Sunday Times 12 June 1988

whether

A letter from a correspondent set me on the trail of some current uses of the word *whether*. She quoted a statement in the 30 April issue of the *Sunday Times*: 'We have to find out why it did not work or whether the operator did something to override it.' 'Overriding,' she pointed out, 'is a possible cause of it not working and therefore the wording should have been "*and* whether"'. So far so good, grammatically at any rate whatever the engineering possibilities were. Then she went on to condemn the parental admonition 'Whether you go to school or whether you don't, you will wear this (pullover, etc.)', which, she said, 'seems a misuse which has the purpose of emphasizing the unimportance of the condition'. A misuse? The command would still have seemed unopposable to the child if '*and* whether' had been used instead, or if the conditional clause had been shortened to 'whether you go to school or not'.

The letter drew me into investigating some other uses of the word *whether*. Traditionally, a *whether . . . or whether* construction introduces (as the *OED* expresses it) a disjunctive clause having a qualifying or conditional force, and standing in adverbial relation to the main sentence, with the meaning 'in either of the cases mentioned, if on the one hand . . . and likewise if on the other hand'. The *OED* gives an example of 1857: 'Whether it is fair, or whether it is not, he pursues his labours with equal success.' To which may be added: 'Whether it was this all too ready confession of mine, or whether he felt the enormity of the crime too great for him to deal with . . . my father did not punish me' (Cecil Day Lewis, 1960). No faults here.

I went on to consider the merits of *whether or not* as against *whether or no*. The *OED* says that the first of these is less frequent than the second and cites examples of *whether or no* from 1650 onward (Addison, Thackeray, and Swinburne, among other writers) to support this view. My more recent evidence points in the opposite direction. *Whether or no* lurks and lingers in nursery rhymes ('A frog he would a-wooing go, Heigh-ho! says Rowley, Whether his mother would let him or no'), and in somewhat self-conscious literary contexts ('depends on whether or no his personal ambition is combined with intellectual ability'—W. H. Auden, 1939). By contrast, *whether or not* (or *whether . . . or not*) abounds in all kinds of writing: 'Whether or not ethyl alcohol can be formed by mammalian tissues has been a controversial topic for many years' (*New Scientist*, 1960); 'She could not decide whether or not to shorten the skirt' (John Wain, 1967); 'But tell me why I care whether this bloke gets his block knocked off by whoever you please or not' (Kingsley Amis, 1988); 'you would not know whether he wore it or not' (Peter Carey, 1988); 'He had not made it plain whether or not I would be welcome on the bus' (Fay Weldon, 1988); 'What authors need to know is whether or not a term has more than one meaning within its subject field' (*International Journal of Lexicography*, 1989). In many contexts the correlative *or not* can be moved from position to position like a fieldsman on a cricket field.

By suppression of the second alternative, *whether* can also be used without a correlative *or* to introduce a simple dependent question. From the Norman Conquest onward, sentences of this type have been used: 'He mette with a poure man . . . & asked hym whether he mette not with a knyghte' (Malory, 1470–85); 'Thither the Londoners flocked . . . to hear whether there was any news' (Macaulay, 1849); 'Barnett was asked whether he thought there'd be goings on' (Penelope Fitzgerald, 1980).

Then there is the question of whether (note the *of*) speakers prefer to place the word *whether* immediately after the word that governs it, or whether a preposition may safely intervene. Examples without an intervening preposition are common: 'I found myself wondering whether I should not try to talk to her' (Jacqueline Simms, 1982); 'it is usually touch and go whether Susie will wait to be seen' (*Encounter*, 1987). Sentences of this type are used all over the English-speaking world: 'Bruce Babbitt . . . said he'll decide Thursday whether to stick with his campaign' (*USA Today*, 1988); 'I looked at Mrs Masson to gauge whether she saw all this' (Thomas Keneally, 1980, Australia); 'She wondered whether I might spare the time to help her close up the house' (C. K. Stead, 1987, New Zealand).

But *whether*-clauses governed by prepositions are also common enough: 'the concern about whether Chinese students stay here or return to China is not ours' (*Bulletin of the American Academy of*

Arts and Sciences, 1987); 'Much will depend on whether Dr Leonard chooses now to concentrate on establishing links with Rome or with Orthodoxy' (*Daily Telegraph*, 1987). No one objects to such preposition-led constructions except in two circumstances: (1) If the governing word happens to be the noun *question*: (with *of*) 'Ms. Frankel raised the question of whether . . . a similar conflict will arise between the urban elites and the peasantry' (*Bulletin of the American Academy of Arts and Sciences*, 1989); (without *of*) 'The question whether to be, or not to be, a career woman had never bothered her' (Doris Lessing, 1988). The *of*-construction and the *of*-less one seem to occur with equal frequency in good writing. (2) Constructions of the type *the question/doubt*, etc. (*as to*) *whether*. The *as to* construction occurs in the Charter of the United Nations (1945): 'In the event of a dispute as to whether the Court has jurisdiction'. But its presence there has done nothing to stop the cold wars of usage guides. Fowler was adamant: 'The question of doubt demands an indirect question in simple apposition . . . The "as to" is not incorrect but merely repulsive.' He is supported by two major usage guides of 1987 and 1988. The latest authority, however, *Webster's Dictionary of English Usage* (1989), says that the omission of *as to* is 'mandatory only if you are writing a telegram'. The battle rumbles on.

Sunday Times 16 July 1989

Index